Classical Chinese Gardens

Edited by Qian Yun
Deputy Managing Editor
China Building Industry Press

Joint Publishing Company, Hongkong
China Building Industry Press, Beijing

Directors:
Yang Jun *(Director, China Building Industry Press)*
Shaw Tze *(Manager, Joint Publishing Co., Hongkong Branch)*

Chief Editor:
Qiao Yun

Executive Editor:
Cheng Liyao

Photographs by:
Yang Gusheng
Chen Xiaoli
Wei Ran

Texts by:
Cheng Liyao

Art Editor:
Yin Jianwen

Design by:
Yau Kam

Layout by:
Holly Liu
Rick Chan

ENGLISH EDITION

Translations by:
Dimon Liu
Chan Chiu Ming

Translation Editor:
Jonathan S. Grant

Edition Editor:
Chan Chiu Ming

Copublished by
Joint Publishing Company (Hongkong Branch)
9 Queen Victoria Street, Hongkong
and
China Building Industry Press
Baiwan Zhuang, Beijing

Distributed by
Joint Publishing Company (Hongkong Branch)

English Edition first published 1982
Reprinted September 1984

Color separation by
Evergreen Photolithography Co.
41 King's Road, 1st Floor, North Point, Hongkong

Printed in Hongkong by
C & C Joint Printing Co. (H.K.) Ltd.
75 Pau Chung Street, Kowloon, Hongkong

ISBN 962.04.0225.1

Contents

Preface

Famous for its landscape scenes, the classical Chinese garden is unique in style. Through a long history of development, the Chinese have established their own distinctive aesthetic theory of garden-making.

The history of the Chinese garden can be traced as far back as the Shang Dynasty (16th-11th century B.C.). In Shang oracle bones, there were numerous inscriptions recording hunts for fun and pleasure. The main hunting ground at the time centered around Yi District, covering present-day southern Shanxi and northern Henan. Later during the Zhou Dynasty special zones for hunting, known as *you,* were designated. Descriptions of these zones can be found in the *Book of Songs (Shi Jing)* where they are called *ling you, ling tai* or *ling chi.*

According to the *Han Zhi Kao (Treatise on Systems of the Han),* the *you* came to be called *yuan* in the Han Dynasty. Besides a hunting ground, the *yuan* also included palaces and pavilions. In fact, in Qin hunting zones, there were already such edifices as the Xing Palace and Chao Palace. The Shang Lin Yuan of Emperor Wu of the Han was stupendous. It comprised a garden, palaces and temples. Inside the *yuan* were reared rare animals and fish as well as deer, dogs, horses and elephants in the midst of flowers and trees. Lakes and ponds were numerous, with Kun Ming Lake being the most famous. A large pleasure ground with buildings forming the main organizational theme, the Shang Lin Yuan is an outstanding example of Qin-Han architectural gardens.

The Jian Zhang Palace, also built by Emperor Wu, was another masterpiece of Han garden-makers. To the north of the palace was the vast Tai Yi Lake with the three islands of Peng Lai, Fang Zhang and Ying Zhou, symbolizing three legendary celestial islands of the same names. Along the banks were a huge stone fish and two tortoises. With ''three islands in a lake'', the Jian Zhang Palace set a pattern for future Chinese gardens.

Between the second and sixth century, the political scene was so corrupt that everyone wanted to escape from worldly affairs and lead a rustic life. Freedom and naturalness became the all-embracing desire. Under the influence of such a social trend, both literature and art underwent significant changes. Aesthetic theories of landscape painting, which were exerting a greater and greater influence on garden design and layout, were also modified. Consequently, a new generation of gardens evolved: the Deer Garden of Northern Wei, the Wriggling Dragon Garden of Later Yan, the Celestial Capital Garden of Northern Qi, the Yuan Pu Garden and Lake East Garden of the Southern Dynasties, etc. ushered in a new epoch of natural landscape gardens. With streams meandering to join lakes and miniature mountains towering in between rare rockeries, palaces and temples, these gardens captured the admiration of everyone. The miniature mountains were completed with peaks and precipices, gorges and valleys as well as streams and cataracts. The trees together with the trailing plants filled the gardens with rustic flavor. The classical man-made structures superimposed on landscape scenes merged the artificial with the natural.

Such an evolution in the landscape garden in turn brought a change in the style of imperial gardens. In the West Garden, Luoyang, built by the order of Emperor Yang of the Sui Dynasty, the traditional feature of ''three islands in a lake'' was preserved. Standing in an artificial lake about ten *li* (one Sui *li* is about 490 meters) in circumference, the legendary islands of Peng Lai, Fang Zhang and Ying Zhou were symbolized by three man-made islands on which were mounted pavilions and temples. From the north a meandering stream flowed through sixteen small gardens before joining the lake. In the overall layout, palaces and pavilions were so designed that they formed a harmonious unity with the surrounding landscape. The West Garden, therefore, could be termed a landscape-architectural garden.

During the Tang and Song dynasties, especially in the magnificent Tang times, Chinese art and literature attained an unprecedented level of achievement. The art of landscape painting also made great advances and the art of Chinese gardens was pushed to a higher aesthetic standard. In the gardens of this new era, the influences of poetry and painting were stronger than ever and the layout emphasized the rendering of a profoundly refined sensibility of conception. As such, the Tang and Song garden came to be called the conceptually allusive landscape garden, a good example of which is the Gen Yue Garden, a model of Northern Song landscape-palatial gardens. On the basis of such an advanced aesthetic skill, Ming and Qing garden-makers built up a sophisticated theory of the garden making art, and their creations became more splendid than ever.

With so many well-noted color pictures, this album would certainly enhance the reader's ability to appreciate this bejeweled area of Chinese building arts. It is my pleasure to write for the album this short account on the history of landscape gardens. An important Chinese cultural legacy, the art of garden-making, I hope, will attract the attention of all.

Wang Juyuan
Vice-chairman of the
Chinese Horticulture Society

The Art of Traditional Chinese Gardens

The design and construction of gardens form an important part of China's cultural traditions, and indeed that of the arts throughout the world. For those who seek to understand traditional Chinese culture, the study of classical gardens is a must.

The origin of traditional gardens can be traced back to the Qin and Han dynasties (c. 221 B.C. to 220 A.D.). By the Tang dynasty (618-907 A.D.) the art had already grown to maturity, embracing now a history of over two thousand years. During this long period of gestation, there has been continuous development in skills and techniques, as well as enrichment in levels of meaning. As a result of international cultural exchange, the Chinese garden tradition has influenced the development of other countries' garden design. For example, the art of garden landscaping was imported into Japan in the sixth century A.D., and has become the germinating source for that country's gardens.

Crystalized from a long history of cultural development, the Chinese garden in its design reflects the predisposition of the Chinese people toward natural beauty, their profound understanding of nature. Comparatively speaking, the Chinese has been one of the earliest peoples to appreciate untrammeled beauty in nature, and has used the inherent forms of nature as guidelines for aesthetics. Chinese traditional gardens differ fundamentally from the geometric formality of Western classical gardens. Noted as one of the most skilful and clever of man-made environments, the Chinese garden specializes in free form, continuous flow, and unexpected twists and turns.

Chinese gardens, in their classic elegance and studied ease reflect the high level of Chinese culture as a whole. Drawing from the aesthetics of architecture, painting, literature, theater, calligraphy and sculpture, they strive for a final synthesizing perfection to create an environment of poetry, the compositional form of painting. Such is the basic formula of garden design. For these very reasons, the traditional gardens still bring forth to the people of today the deep enjoyment and power of an artistic experience. We can discover from this treasure trove many valuable aesthetic theories and practical techniques.

The process of making gardens has a very close connection with the traditional art of ink and wash landscape paintings. From the very beginning they developed symbiotically, unlike the garden parks of Europe where painting and the art of garden landscaping did not come together until the eighteenth century. Chinese gardens were mostly created by poets and painters who sought an atmosphere of poetic and painterly feeling. In appreciating these gardens, one can easily imagine them in terms of contemplative nature poems and the slow unfolding of a Chinese painted scroll.

In Chinese gardens the most expressive and characteristic feature is the miniature mountains. In the vast stretches of China's countryside there are many famous mountains which have served as an unending source of inspiration for garden-makers. Similarly, China enjoys an abundance of many unusual rock formations, and garden-makers have utilized different shapes, colors and textures, indeed the natural essence of rocks to create cliffs, peaks, valleys, grottoes and caves in unending variations of miniature mountains. Through these spectacular forms which inspire an association with the famous, majestic mountain ranges, the ambience of being in real nature is created. Reminiscent of the Chinese painterly method, which required only "a foot to create whole mountains and forests", this landscaping mode shrinks the vastness of Nature in order to enhance the appreciation and comprehension of it through art. This symbolic representationalism is the most characteristic feature of the art of Chinese gardens. It differs from the Western tradition of realism, for it embodies the special attraction and power of theater.

Architecture enjoys full expression and development in Chinese gardens for, compared with Western gardens, those of China contain and give more importance to buildings. The architecture in these gardens becomes part and parcel of the whole landscape composition. Buildings provide the focal points from which the garden landscape is appreciated as well as places for rest and recreation. As the architecture is designed to fit in with the tone and setting of the landscape, various and unusual forms of architectural construction are used — *tíng* (pavilion), *xiè* (pavilion or house on a terrace), *láng* (porch), *qiáo* (bridge), *fáng* (stone boat), *fāng* (archway), *tīng* (hall), *táng* (great hall), *lóu* (two-storied hall), *gé* (two-storied pavilion), etc. The architectural styles in Chinese gardens, in terms of floor plans, roof shapes, form and position of doors and windows, wall surfaces, frescoes and sculpture all possess special characteristics and unending variations. Nevertheless, they harmonize with the overall composition and do not hinder the main theme of the garden.

Water constitutes a feature of Chinese gardens that cannot be missed. From enormous man-made lakes to dainty ponds, water forms the major thematic element of garden composition. In the treatment of the water surface area and the shoreline, a perfectly natural effect is sought. Geometric ponds are seldom found in Chinese gardens, but where such a shape complements the theme it is employed. In contrast to Western gardens which use the motion of water, such as in fountains, to express a joyful and scintillating atmosphere, the essential element in the treatment of water in Chinese gardens is stillness. In its calmness and quietude, water establishes a contemplative and peaceful aura.

Another component part of the Chinese garden is the paired couplet which typically appears on building columns and lintel tablets. These make up the major decorative element of the buildings. Carved on tablets, these poetic lines indicate a special landscape theme, or the source of the garden-maker's imaginative inspiration, or perhaps express the owner's interests and temperament. Thus while wandering through a garden, the visitor can also appreciate the artistic culture of calligraphy, carving, and poetry. Chinese gardens can be grouped under three main categories: the imperial gardens, the private gardens and the grand natural landscape gardens, this last type consisting mostly of temples, monasteries and ancestral hall gardens. These all differ greatly in size, theme, and characteristics. Because most imperial gardens are situated in the North, a certain grandness, formality and classicism has become characteristic of Northern gardens. In the South gardens typically were private, the most famous of them being located in Suzhou (Soochow), specially noted for their unpredictability in layout, and profound tranquility in atmosphere. In many scenic areas grand landscape gardens comprising tourist spots, temples and ancestral halls were formed after many years of development. These gardens use the natural environment as a backdrop and add here and there man-made features to complement the overall composition. These gardens are much more rustic and natural in comparison with the other two types.

Because the major construction material is wood, many Chinese gardens were destroyed by the depredations of time, natural disaster and war. The ones that have been preserved consist mainly of those constructed during the Ming and Qing dynasties. Still, from these we can glimpse the great art of traditional Chinese gardens.

Imperial Gardens

The Chinese garden, not unlike those of other ancient countries, has its origin in imperial gardens. Gardens can only develop after the economy of society has reached a level where wealth has been concentrated in the hands of the governing elite. With this vast wealth, they created magnificent gardens.

From historical records, ancient paintings and literature, the earliest indications of gardens are found in the Qin and Han dynasties. The First Emperor of Qin built a garden named the Shang Lin Yuan south of the River Wei, in which was constructed the Epang Palace. This is the earliest imperial garden recorded in history. The first emperor of the Han Dynasty, Gao Zu, built the Wei Yang Palace along with the famous lake Tai Yi. In the midst of the lake the artificial islands Peng Lai, Fang Zhang and Ying Zhou were constructed, symbolizing three heavenly islands. Han Wu Di renovated the Shang Lin Yuan and added to it the Jian Zhang Palace as well as Kun Ming Lake. The Shang Lin Yuan occupied an area of several hundred square *li* (one Han *li* is about 400 meters). There were ten clusters of palaces. Within the garden there were all kinds of animals, unusual flowers and plants. The vastness of size can be imagined. At this time, the important feature of the imperial garden was the symbolic composition of ''three islands in a lake''. From this was established the basic compositional theme of imperial gardens, which all the later imperial gardens imitated.

During the Wei and Jin dynasties there were continuous wars. The people were plunged into disaster but the governing aristocrats still lived in excessive luxury and had lots of gardens built. Emperor Wen of the Wei Dynasty built the famous Fragrant Forest Garden in Luoyang, the capital, and using stones taken from Tai Xing Mountain he had the well-known Jing Yang Mountain made in the garden.

During the Northern and Southern Dynasties (420-581) the building of gardens became even more fashionable. In the North, imperial gardens imitated basically the characteristics of the Qin and Han dynasties, but in the South the art of garden-making was much influenced by the social thoughts of the Western Jin (265-316) as well as its literature and fine arts. The intelligentsia of the time were enthralled by Taoism, Buddhism and occultism, and every scholar amused himself with discourse on the metaphysical and mysterious. Living amidst the mountains detached from worldly affairs was the ideal of these intellectuals. Under the influence of such an atmosphere, the art of garden-making in the South turned toward the pursuit of nature and the contemplative spirit. Emperor Wen of the (Liu) Song dynasty built a garden by Lake Sang in the Jian Kang area (present-day Lake Xuan Wu in Nanjing). By comparison, this garden had few buildings and was dominated mostly by the unaltered elements of nature.

During the Sui and Tang dynasties, the feudal system was most prosperous and dynamic. This was also the time when various Chinese arts matured, and the imperial garden experienced great development. The Sui emperor Wen Di built the Western Garden which was approximately 200 square *li* (one Sui *li* is about 500 meters) in size. The lake in the garden was about ten *li* in circumference, with three ''heavenly'' islets in the middle. In this enormous and splendid garden, there were sixteen clusters of buildings, crisscrossing canals, flying bridges, and bamboo and willows as well as clumps of flowers everywhere. The dragon boat in the lake could get to every part of the garden by way of the canals.

The Tang Dynasty was even more prosperous. Emperor Xuan Zong's travel lodge, the Hua Qing (Magnificent Clear) Palace, was very famous. The natural surroundings of the area were unsurpassed, and were further beautified by the hot springs nearby, which turned the area into a very special palace retreat. The imperial family could no longer be satisfied with palaces and gardens within the confines of the imperial city walls, and had to seek further enjoyment in such a natural environment. The famous Tang poet, Du Mu, in describing the Hua Qing Palace, wrote:

> ''Back now in the capital, I am
> Still entranced by the beauty
> Of the Hua Qing Palace.
> Sprawling like an embroidery,
> Thousands of halls stand proudly
> One after the other in magnificence.''

This vividly indicates the extravagance and grandness of the imperial travel lodge.

To seek naturally odd and unusually shaped rocks and to have them placed in chosen spots within the gardens became an especially popular trend during Song times. During the Northern Song Dynasty, Emperor Hui Zong was so enraptured by literature and the fine arts that he totally neglected state affairs and lost China to the barbarians. He spent ten years building Golden Brightness Lake at Bian Liang, the imperial city, and created the famous Longevity Mountain as well as peak Gen Yue on it. He did not hesitate to break up bridges and destroy roads and canals in order to ship these rocks to Bian Liang. This was the notorious affair of the "mass transportation of flowers and rocks". Even these days we can still glimpse some of these rocks scattered in other gardens, as Emperor Hui Zong's garden was destroyed along with his empire.

Longevity Mountain covered an area of approximately ten square *li.* The highest peak, Gen Yue, reached 150 meters in height. The range of mountains ran from east to west. The eastern area of the garden was a plum forest. There existed in the garden not only the landscapes imitating nature, but also artificial valleys, lakes, streams and stylistically placed pavilions scattered over the garden for the observation of scenic vistas from special vantage points. As evidenced by the construction of Longevity Mountain, the art of designing gardens, as well as the skills used in executing these designs, had reached a new peak. The technique of layering the miniauture mountain attained an unprecedented level of development.

The Liao, Jin, Yuan and Ming dynasties did not build many imperial gardens. The main one was the Western Garden in imperial Beijing (present-day North Sea, Middle Sea and South Sea). During the Qing Dynasty the interest in garden-making reached a new height. Qing imperial gardens had many variations, unlike the familiar standard types. Within the Forbidden City there were four little gardens: the Royal Garden, Fortune Seeking Garden, Kindness-Tranquility Garden and Qian Long Memorial Garden. Within the imperial city the three lakes, the North Sea, Middle Sea and South Sea, were enlarged. In the western suburb of Beijing, there were such beautiful gardens as the Yuan Ming, Chang Chun, Qing Yi, Jing Ming and Jing Yi. About 200 kilometers north of Beijing was the Chengde district where the Imperial Summer Resort was built. These imperial gardens, spreading over various spots, served to entertain the royal family at different times.

The Qing Dynasty improved greatly the art of garden-making. Emperors Kang Xi and Qian Long both traveled to the south numerous times and imported to the north many southern garden techniques. The most impressive and largest among the Qing imperial gardens was the Yuan Ming. Known as the "Garden of gardens", the Yuan Ming was situated in the northwest suburb of Beijing. Built in the forty-eighth year of the reign of Kang Xi, it was a grand landscape garden constructed completely on level land, comprising scores of scenic fairylands. Each scenic area had its own clusters of buildings. The number of buildings, as well as the complexity and variety of landscapes, were virtually unprecedented. This magnificent garden was destroyed in 1860 by French and British armies. That was indeed an irreparable loss to the heritage of garden-making.

In retrospect, we can see a continuous development and improvement in the art of garden-making throughout the past two thousand years, and the achievements of Chinese garden-makers can be said to be glorious. The composition of imperial gardens clearly reflected the considered specialisation of functions. Within the gardens were an administration court, living quarters and recreation areas, each serving different purposes. Temples were also included in the Qing imperial gardens, adding to them a special religious air. Through this, the imperial family's claim to its ruling divinity was expressed. In the main, the imperial garden's most salient artistic feature was that of dignified grandiosity. Due to changes in the socio-economic conditions and influenced by developments in other forms of art, the aesthetic of the imperial garden also evolved. Once emphasizing formality and dignity with all the buildings packed together, the imperial garden gradually became more like a landscape garden with nature as its model.

Because architecture assumed a very important position in the garden, the placement of the buildings in the imperial gardens formed the backbone of the designs. In the traditional courtyard compounds, the buildings were organized on a north-south axis, and the imperial garden utilized this principle. In the large imperial gardens, there was always a main north-south axis linking all the important clusters of buildings, while the secondary axes linked lesser buildings of various sizes and functions. The lesser buildings were usually situated in the midst of a natural landscape, seeking to balance and juxtapose the formality of the main axis and make a harmonious overall composition. In each cluster, the buildings were oriented inwards, forming an independent entity within the natural landscape. The making of the whole garden utilized man-made elements along with natural elements to create a balanced and harmonious whole of scenic beauty.

The imperial gardens were not as formal and solemn as the imperial palaces. In plan and shape, they were freer, and generally there was no hierachical organization. The imposing *wudian* style roof (hipped roof with highly elaborated ridges) was seldom included; the yellow glazed tiles were limited to the most important building within the garden and the majority of the buildings used gray tiles. The basic color composition thus consisted of green trees, red columns and gray roof tops. The atmosphere was clear and bright, rich and elegant. The fresco was a major feature of the imperial garden. In order to create a vivacious and relaxed atmosphere, the serene *hexi* style with dragon designs and heavy colors was avoided. The *suzhi* style, which consisted of landscape embellished with allegorical fables and flowers and trees, was adopted.

Because of the scale of imperial gardens was so vast, the sizes of miniature mountains and man-made lakes were also considerable, all to satisfy the pleasures and whims of the governing regime. Mountain and water are the backbone of the garden. Together they mark the garden's profile and define the organization of the whole compound. In the lake there are always islets, a treatment rooted in the ancient dictum that an imperial garden must have "three islands in one lake". By the Ming and Qing era, however, the dictum was not followed too strictly.

Full of artistic values and refinement, minor architectural objects such as pagodas, memorial arches, railings and balustrades, stone tablets, sculptures of animals, partition walls and stone bridges were also important features in the imperial garden. Forming the centerpoints in courtyards, and establishing juxtapositing points, they open new vistas and add much to making the gardens more lively and more interesting.

Existing imperial gardens include Beijing's Bei Hai Park, the Summer Palace and the Royal Garden with the Forbidden City, the Imperial Summer Resort in Chengde district, and the Magnificent Clear Lake in Lintong district, Shaanxi Province. These gardens include the examples of gardens within the Forbidden City proper, gardens in the suburb of the imperial city, and gardens for the monarch in retreat. They are fine examples of the imperial garden, with invaluable artistic qualities.

Private Gardens

Private gardens arose later than those of imperial patronage. The earliest historical records come from the Han Dynasty, and from that time onwards each dynasty developed and improved on this art form. During the Ming and Qing dynasties the fever for constructing private gardens reached its peak, and a great number were built. The association of gardens with painting and literature became increasingly important, and the artistry and skills employed in forming the gardens reached a very high level. During the Ming and Qing, the Suzhou gardens were the most renowned for their elegance and sophistication. Even internationally, these gardens acquired a high standing, and the Suzhou garden is considered the pearl of this Chinese art.

The most famous private garden of Han Dynasty records was built in Luoyang by a rich man, Yuan Guanghan.The area of the garden was approximately three hectares. Meandering corridors ran through it, with pavilions dotting the landscape in convenient places. Scattered between there were rockeries and clear water ponds, as well as a well stocked zoo and much unusual flora and fauna.

During the Wei and Jin dynasties, the houses of mandarins had gardens in the back of their living quarters. Mountains were constructed, ponds excavated, islands created in the ponds, and pavilions built in different spots. The best known gardens of that era were Luxuriant Forest Garden, Zhang Lun's Garden and Eastern Xiang Garden in Luoyang. This was the time when the art of "piling mountains" become sophisticated. The "mountains" were modeled after those in nature, with enormorous rocks creating unusual peaks and spectacular cliffs through which rugged and steep stone paths led. Many mandarins and scholars were passionate in expressing their love for nature, creating a trend in Chinese cultural history that valued highly this aesthetic of beauty. Many of these well-known personages retired from the wordly life to lead that of a hermit. The trend has profound influences on the art of garden-making and the development of gardens has been moving in the direction of imitating nature ever since.

During the Sui and Tang periods, the powerful mandarins followed the traditions of garden-making established during the Northern and Southern Dynasties. Because of the prosperity of the times, wealth increased in the hands of individuals, and private gardens became bigger. The famous poetry of the Tang Dynasty reached its apogee, and the romanticism of the poets blended harmoniously with the art of garden-making and brought vitality to its development. Many of these great poets felt passionate love for nature, for "retiring" into the countryside, living in thatched huts and building their own gardens.

Wang Chuan Villa, built by the famous poet Wang Wei, was the most well-known garden of the time. Located within the famous and beautiful Zhong Nan Peaks, Wang utilized the natural setting, adding a small amount of the human touch, thus creating a garden of special elegance. It was comparable to a landscape painting in the impressionistic style. Poetic names were used for specially created scenes, for example, "Willow Waves", "Melody Lake", and "Dainty Apricot Hostel". Intellectuals and scholars made an influential mark on the design of the gardens by pioneering the art of blending the natural with the man-made. This was a pivotal time in garden development.

During the Song Dynasty, commercial and handicraft activities increased substantially. The population grew quickly, bringing people together in greater proximity as the size and number of cities expanded. Mandarins and relations of the imperial family as well as wealthy merchants wanted to enjoy the convenience of city life while at the same time tasting the sweet scent of mountain greenery. They therefore continued and developed the tradition of building gardens alongside living quarters, creating what became known as "urban mountain forest".

At the time, the Eastern Capital of Kaifeng and the Western Capital of Luoyang were the largest and most prosperous cities. According to historical records, there were in Luoyang over one thousand households with private gardens, of which some twenty were truly notable. In Kaifeng there were not less than a dozen famous gardens. In the south, private gardens were concentrated around Pingjiang (present-day Suzhou), Wuxing, and Lin'an (present-day Hangzhou).

The size of private gardens at that time was very large, with flowers and trees planted everywhere. Ponds and bamboo groves, pavilions and lofty houses as well as earth mounts were constructed.

The number of structures in the gardens also increased to provide the owners with various spots for different kinds of entertainment. In composing the plan, theories of ''juxtaposing views'' and ''borrowing views'' were applied so as to include visually the natural scenery from afar into the total picture of the garden, thus rendering a grand impression. It became popular to create unusual mountains with such formations as spectacular peaks, hanging cliffs, brooks, valleys and caves. The appreciation of rocks was already a kind of genteel hobby. Placed in singular positions they were known as the lonely rocks or the odd peaks as determined by their shapes and sizes. The man-made dimension was increased and the level of artistry enhanced.

Because the dynasties of Liao, Jin, Yuan, Ming and Qing all had their capital in Beijing, the gathering of mandarins quickly made Beijing a city of many famous gardens. During the Ming Dynasty, there were over 20 well-known private gardens in the suburbs of Beijing. The most famous of these was Mi Wanzhong's Dipper Garden (Shao Yuan). During the Qing Dynasty, there were no less than fifty gardens built of which, however, only seven or eight are preserved to this day, the main ones being Prince Gong's Palace, Ke Garden, Nuo Tong's Mansion, and Liu Yong's Residence. These gardens often changed owners, and many were left in disrepair, or reconstructed for other purposes. As a result, the original designs were totally changed.

At the time, the Southern gardens clustered around prosperous cities which enjoyed good communications, mild weather and an advanced level of cultural attainment. Among the most important cities where private gardens abounded were Yangzhou, Nanjing, Suzhou, Jiaqing and Hangzhou.

During the early Qing Dynasty, Yangzhou, being situated at the crossroad of the Grand Canal and the Yangtze river, monopolized the salt trade and became exceptionally prosperous. It was a city of wealthy merchants, as well as scholars and noblemen. Even Emperor Qian Long, in his many trips to the south, passed through Yangzhou. As a result, many began to build gardens to vie for the privilege of hosting the emperor. If the emperor stayed at the garden, or left a poem behind, the importance of the host would be elevated and the garden would rocket in value.

Most of the gardens were built in the forest area around Slender West Lake. They not only ''borrowed views'' from the lake and the forest; they also borrowed views from each other, creating a situation that never existed before. On the whole, these gardens were not for residences. They were used for social gatherings, drinking and writing poems, singing and dancing as well as relaxing. They were often opened in the morning for the public to visit. There were no less than a hundred such gardens, the eight most famous of which were Shadow Garden, Garden of Wang the Equerry, Bian's Garden, Round Garden, East Garden, Charming Spring Garden, South Garden and Dwarf Bamboo Garden.

Gardens in Yangzhou were famous for their technique of layering rocks to form mountains. At the climax of this vogue, almost every family in Yangzhou had designed its own rockeries amidst pools of water in a misty background with pavilions standing in solitude. But when the Qing Emperor Dao Guang came to the throne, the once prosperous Yangzhou began a rapid decline. The melody of music and dance waned, and the art of garden-making withered. The gardens that were preserved can be counted on one hand, but even from these few, we can still see how the art of garden-making once prospered.

The Suzhou private garden has a very long history. From the time of the Five Dynasties (907-960) to the middle of the Qing Dynasty, the Suzhou garden experienced an uninterrrupted development. Handicraft industries and commercial activities in Suzhou were most prosperous, adding to the city's wealth until it became the largest and richest city south of the Yangtze River. Besides, Suzhou had superior natural features for making gardens. Canals criss-crossed within the city, and this plentiful source of water provided easy transport and beautiful scenery. Nearby, there were many quarries of rocks, and a great variety of plants and flowers could be found.

These factors, taken together, made Suzhou a place for merchants as well as painters and poets, and contributed to the development of the art of garden-making. Mandarins and wealthy merchants vied for land and made these gardens into leisure centers where they chanted their poems and composed paintings, or made them into elegant retirement paradises for their later years in life.

Suzhou has preserved more classical gardens than any other city in China. These gardens are furthermore of the highest quality and artistry, the famous ones including Garden of the Unsuccessful Politician (Zhuo Zhen Garden), Lingering Garden (Liu Garden), Garden of the Master of the Fishing Nets (Wang Shi Garden), Lion Grove Garden (Shi Zi Lin) and Surging Wave Pavilion (Cang Lang Ting). As can be seen from these gardens, the special qualities of the Suzhou garden lie in the twists and turns in plan as well as the unfathomable mysterious atmosphere. Full of unpredictable variations, with poetic elegance and painterly effects, they are the most preeminent of the Southern gardens, commanding great influence over all China. Suzhou garden architecture is specially known for its beautiful forms and fine decorative carvings. Stone mountains, large bodies of water, and flowers and woods are all balanced just right. In the art of ''creating mountain and forest in a foot of space'', the Suzhou style reached the highest artistry.

Private gardens of the south are normally situated behind or beside the living quarters. While the various parts of the living quarters are grouped together around a central axis creating a formal order of halls and chambers, the gardens are free and asymmetrical in plan. This posed a delightfully contrasting yet harmonious view. In composition, there is normally one large open space in which the main scenes as well as the main viewing pavilion are staged. Around the main open core are various smaller spaces. Partitioned by corridors and walls, the central open and the minor closed spaces are connected visually by windows and cave gates. In the large gardens, the main open core is often decorated with incidental architecture, trees and rockeries to form many spatial twists and turns, making it even more mysterious and serene.

The main structures within the gardens are built for hosting parties and receiving guests. Such might be a pavilion overlooking a water surface or a spacious chamber which is open on all sides so that the guests could enjoy the surrounding sceneries. The vistas are composed of the rockeries, trees and water which are so designed and arranged that they orchestrate a view comparable to a landscape painting. Thus, the aesthetics of landscape painting are observed, along with the taste of the owner as well as considerations of the landform setting. Following the forms of well-known actual mountains the larger earth and rock hillocks are composed of peaks and cliffs, with twisting paths for climbing up and down. The smaller miniature mountains consist solely of rocks, placed in the limited spaces and intended for viewing only.

The bodies of water are usually free form in shape, while the stone edge of the pond follows a naturally meandering aesthetic. From this we can see the great influence of Chinese landscape paintings. Sometimes the rim of a podium or terrace overlooking the water is utilized to form an edge of the pond. The resultant straight line thus forms a graceful contrast to the natural bends of the pool. With small bridges, floating pavilions and rockeries located over and in the water, the pool seems a vast space with no boundaries. There are few plants by the water's edge, but there are often water lilies and water hyacinth floating placidly in the water. From outside the garden, water flows elegantly in a leisurely and quiet manner through the various open spaces before passing on; there are no fast running cataracts in most Chinese gardens. The body of serene water, like a mirror, gives a clear reflection of scenery and buildings so that the garden appears to be much more spacious than it actually is, bestowing it with a graceful and much sought after tranquility.

The buildings in the private garden of the south occupy more space than their counterparts in the north. The plans and elevations of the architecture vary, but generally speaking all appear graceful, free and vivacious. These buildings are often connected by meandering porches, forming an organic compound. The porches also provide shelter from showers and gusts as well as the hot burning sun. These structures, combined in different ways with trees and rockeries as well as man-made mountains, produce a rich variety of settings which make up a prominent feature of the gardens of the south.

Furthermore, the varied shapes and artistry of lattice windows and cave gates, the symbolic cloud walls, the mosaics of natural pebble paving, the poems and calligraphy displayed on columns and lintel tablets, the fine and archaic furniture, the carvings on balustrades and podia, and the other architectural decorations all contribute to a very clear and fresh beauty.

Natural Scenic Parks and Temple Gardens

The Chinese people have a history of appreciating and enjoying nature's beauty. Many natural scenic areas have long been utilized as parks and have attracted numerous tourists. Those scenic areas, often including many beautiful gardens, that were either close to populous cities or blessed with convenient transportation, were chosen to be developed. These scenic parks differ from the previous two types of gardens in which the man-made elements dominate. But these parks cannot be considered as totally natural environments either, for they were designed with nature as the basic setting, adding man-made elements at crucial points, uniting natural works with human endeavors, resulting in parks that are unique in character. The process is like choosing a piece of natural jade, then polishing some parts, sculpturing others, yet leaving most of the jade untouched in order to blend artfully the existing natural qualities with novel constructs.

The traditional scenic parks differ substantially from the imperial and private gardens. They were designed for public recreation. During the Tang Dynasty, such a scenic park was situated southeast of the Tang capital Chang'an. This is probably the earliest recorded example. The Meandering River (Qu Jiang) Scenic Region, as this place was known, was famous for its extraordinary beauty. Within its area, many viewing pavilions, rest hostels, palaces, lofts, and pagodas were built to facilitate the enjoyment of nature. At that time, the common people and the mandarins, as well as the imperial family went to this spot for recreation.

As famous tourist attractions, the natural scenic parks all contain scenes of exceptional beauty. These scenes, known as *jing,* are usually given poetic names. Typically, there are many different scenes in each park, for instance, the eight scenes of the Great Brightness Lake, Jinan, the ten famous scenes of West Lake, Hangzhou, and the 24 scenes of Slender West Lake, Yangzhou. At one time there were as many as 60 scenes in Foolish Old Man Valley of Wuxi. These settings are always beautiful, unusual and spectacular, often including natural grottoes, spring creeks and waterfalls. At the best spots for enjoying the landscapes, lofts, pavilions, or pagodas were built. The planning and design of these structures were geared towards utilizing and displaying the specialities of the parks, with pavilions sited beside grottoes, viewing lofts set against cliffs, and ponds created by embanking the springs. Unlike the other two types of gardens, there were no set rules and models to follow, so the site became the main determinant.

Many old Chinese temples and ancestral halls were situated in scenic areas as beautiful as paintings. The existence of these temples and halls promoted the development of the surrounding landscape. The temples and ancestral halls that were built within the city limits did not often have gardens, but in scenic spots these buildings were embraced by nature and the architecture was designed to blend with the environment. They themselves became areas for relaxation and sightseeing.

The development of the natural scenic parks has very close associations with famous historical figures, poets, painters and calligraphers. These historical figures often left behind traces of their visits, in poems or in their calligraphy. Quite often, a famous poet or painter came upon a hitherto untouched scenic area and initiated its development. Their works glorified the natural beauty of the area, making it well-known to the public. In commemoration of these historical figures, later generations often had their poems and calligraphy inscribed on stones and wood, placing these on pavilions or viewing platforms and incorporating them into an essential part of the overall design. These signs enriched the meaning and historical importance of the parks, adding to the interests of potential visitors. For those who visit these scenic parks, a close and tangible contact with history and historical figures keeps one aware of the richness of Chinese culture, and arouses feelings of cultural pride. For example, in Wuxi's Foolish Old Man Valley, the famous calligrapher Wang Xizhi's handwriting of *Preface to the Orchid Pavilion Collection* is inscribed on stones and placed in the Arhat Pavilion. In Taiyuan the *Epigraph on the Memorial Temple of Jin* and its *Preface,* done in the calligraphy of the great Tang emperor Tai Zong, is a treasure. In West Lake the Tomb of Yue Fei, a Southern Song hero, is situated. Almost all the ancient scenic parks have preserved some valuable historical relics; this is peculiar to traditional scenic parks of China.

Fairy tales and legends handed down for several thousand years often lie behind these traditional scenic parks. When visitors come to these parks, it is natural that they associate these legends and fairy tales with the areas, and even specially seek their signs and relics. This increases the interest and adds to the mystical aura of these scenic parks. For example, the famous fairy tale ''The Legend of the White Snake'' had supposedly taken place in Zhenjiang's Golden Mount, where the Temple of the Monk Fa Hai (the hero of the Legend) and the White Snake Cave are located. In Nanjing, Mochou Lake was named after a common woman of one thousand and four hundred years ago, whose moving love story lives to this day. In Hangzhou's West Lake, there are the ''Broken Bridge'' and ''Jumping Tiger'', both of which are associated with ancient legends.

The scenic parks are where the ancient people went for recreation and the enjoyment of natural landscapes, as well as for the worship of their gods. The time for religious ceremonies, cultural performances and market gatherings was simultaneously the time when most people went to the parks for sightseeing. Whenever the wind was gentle and the sun warm, the common people would come by the thousands to join in the festivities. These activities grant a special color to Chinese natural scenic parks.

Unlike the other two types of gardens, the natural scenic parks are not constructed according to a master plan nor with a preconceived program. Built gradually, they are developed over a long period of time. Therefore, we can see within a single park designs and styles of different periods. The built structures of these parks normally only use construction material of the immediate locality. As such, they are not as sophisticated as those in the imperial gardens and private gardens for which great quantities of special stones and wood from distant areas were imported. The architecture in the scenic park remains freer, simpler, more plain and clear of decoration. They excel in rustic beauty.

Because the scenic parks are more public in nature, their preservation has confronted great difficulties. Often they prospered and declined with the ups and downs of a dynasty, falling into disrepair when the dynasty came to an end. Therefore many no longer exist, though quite a few of them were repaired by later generations and are thus preserved. Most of the extant scenic parks are from the Qing Dynasty, of which many have been refurbished and reconstructed by the People's Republic.

Imperial Gardens

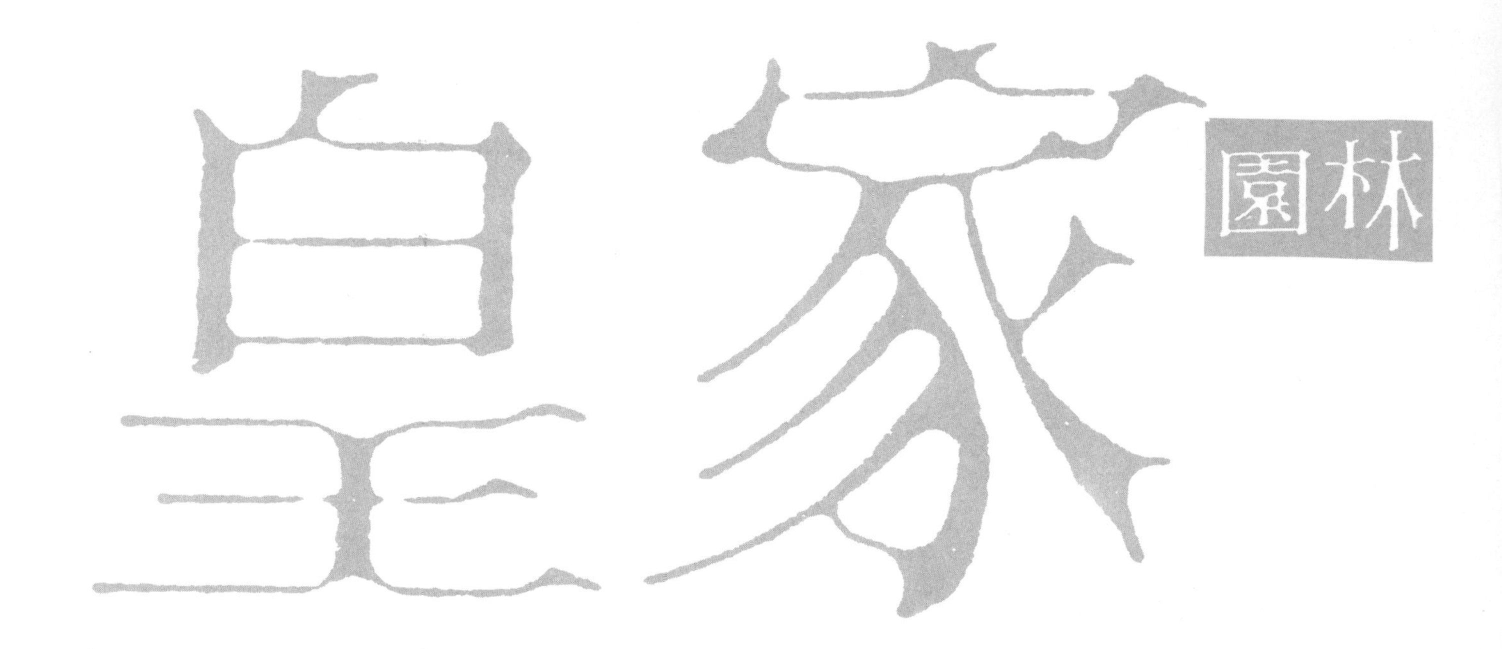

Bei Hai Park

Situated west of the Forbidden City and Jing Hill, Bei Hai has been an imperial garden from the Jin Dynasty through Qing times (1179-1911), thus enjoying a history today of over eight hundred years. In 1179 the Jin emperor Shi Zong excavated a huge lake and made use of the earth thus obtained to create an artificial island. The lake came to be called Bei Hai (North Sea) and the island Qiong Hua (Resplendent Jade). Erected on Qiong Hua Island was a stupendous detached palace. For decoration, the Taihu eroded limestones displayed in the Gen Yue Garden of the Bianjing, former capital of the Northern Song Dynasty, were removed to the island. On the peak, the Moon Palace (Guang Han Gong) offered a panoramic view of the surroundings. In 1260, Kublai Khan resided in the Moon Palace and renamed the island Longevity Hill (Wan Shou Shan) and the lake Tai Yi. The island, as the imperial seat now, became the focal point of the layout of the Grand Capital (modern Beijing). The whole complex underwent a large-scale extension during the Qian Long period of the Qing and most existing buildings were constructed at that time.

Qiong Hua Island, as the island is commonly called, has a circumference of 1,193 meters and rises 32.8 meters high. It is the main sector of Bei Hai Park while the 35.9 meter high White Dagoba on its peak is the center of the complex's layout.

Descending from White Dagoba, Shan Yin Hall with its glazed roof, Universal Peace Hall, Enlightenment Hall, Cloudy Greeny Archway and Everlasting Peace Stone Bridge line the southern slope of the island and join Round City (Tuan Cheng) further south, forming the main axis of the 68.2 hectare complex.

Along the western slope, Jade Hall (Lin Guang Dian) and the Chamber of Reading the Classics (Yue Gu Lou) are the principal structures. Housed in the Chamber of Reading the Classics are stone inscriptions of the calligraphy of the great calligraphers Wang Xizhi, Wang Xianzhi and Wang Xun. Spreading over the slope are rockeries, pavilions and halls: Mu Jian House, Cloud Mist Pavilion (Yanyun Jintai Ting), Crystal Region, Sweet Dew Hall, Pan Qing House and Bowing to Mount Pavilion (Yi Shan Ting) are the most elegant structures.

Standing by the coast of the north slope, the semicircular Yan Mansion offers a view of White Dagoba to its south and a panaroma of the vast "North Sea" lake to the north. Ripple Hall (Yi Lan Tang) and Serene Way Studio (Dao Ning Zhai) in the middle are two famous pavilions. Rising and falling along the slope, Drunk with the Classics Hall, Describing the Wonders Stone House, Breezy Elegant House, House Amidst the Greenery, Pavilion of the Universe Embodied in a Jar, Little Kunyou Pavilion together make a spectacular scene.

On the eastern slope is another group of buildings, with the Gate Leading onto the Mount (Zhi Shan Men), stone bridge, archway and Pearl of Wisdom Hall making a minor axis. To the north of Pearl of Wisdom Hall is Sighting the Spring Pavilion (Jian Chun Ting). Further north, a stone tablet with the inscriptions "Qiong Dao Chun Yin (Qiong Hua Island in Spring)" marks one of the eight best scenes in ancient Beijing.

Besides the buildings on the island, there are still numerous structures in Bei Hai Park. These are concentrated along the east and north coasts of the North Sea. The waterside hall Hao Pu Jian on the east coast stretches out onto a pool of water with peculiarly shaped rockeries rising from it. To the north of the pavilion is the Painted Boat Studio. On the north coast is a delightful garden called Mirror Clear Studio which had been the residence of the Qing crown princes when they visited the park. The north is noted for its religious buildings such as the Little West Land, Chan Fu Temple, Great West Land and the Pure Land. To the west of Little West Land is the meticulously carved Nine Dragon Wall. In front of Chan Fu Temple, the Five Dragon Pavilions jut out onto the water,

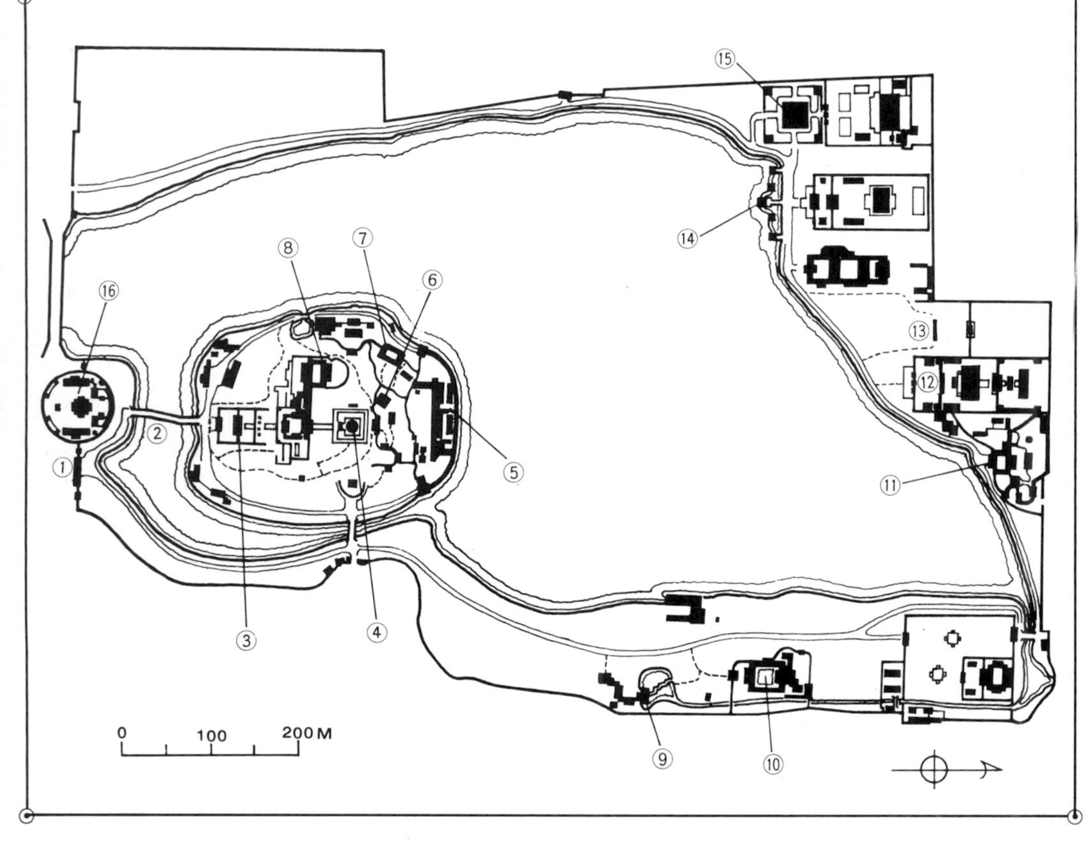

Bei Hai Park
1. *entrance*
2. *Everlasting Peace Bridge*
3. *Everlasting Peace Temple*
4. *White Dagoba*
5. *Ripple Hall*
6. *Drunk With the Classics Hall*
7. *Chamber of Reading of the Classics*
8. *Qing Xiao Mansion*
9. *Hao Pu Jian waterside pavilion*
10. *Painted Boat Studio*
11. *Mirror Clear Studio*
12. *West Land*
13. *Nine Dragon Wall*
14. *Five Dragon Pavilions*
15. *Pure Land*
16. *Round City*

3

4

5

6

1. *White Dagoba and other structures forming the main axis of the park.*
2. *A view of the Qiong Hua Island*
3. *A panoramic view of the Five Dragon Pavilions. The pavilions used to be the place where Qing emperors watched fireworks displays during the Chinese New Year.*
4. *Han Gu Hall, an enclosed garden court northwest of the White Dagoba.*
5. *Stone path in the backyard of Painted Boat Studio*
6. *"Qiong Hua Island in Spring", the tablet marking one of the eight best scenes in ancient Beijing. The inscription is in the handwriting of Emperor Qian Long.*

8

9

7. *A distant view of Hao Pu Jian. An open hall standing over the water, it is connected to the park entrance by a stone bridge.*
8. *A view of the open hall on Refreshing Lake Walkway. In the distance is a little stone bridge spanning over the lake.*
9. *Section of the Nine Dragon Wall*
10. *The open hall on Refreshing Lake Walkway in the garden court of Jing Qing Studio.*

10

11

12

11. Inside view of Painted Boat Studio. Square in plan, it is a garden court with its built structures enclosing a lotus pool in the center.

12. Color paintings on the architrave panels of the Refreshing Lake Walkway

13. The little stone bridge with Climbing Hill Walkway and the open hall of Yan Hua Xuan in its background.

Summer Palace

Located about ten kilometers northwest of the city proper of Beijing, the Summer Palace (Yi He Yuan) was called Weng Shan Bo in Yuan times. During the Ming Dynasty, Yuan Jing Temple was constructed on this site. A large-scale reconstruction took place in Qing times when Emperor Qian Long ordered the excavation of a lake and formation of a hill on its east bank. The hill became Longevity Hill (Wan Shou Shan) and the lake Kun Ming. Yuan Jing Temple was extended by adding pavilions, terraces and halls to the existing structure. The enlarged complex, renamed Clear Ripple Garden (Qing Yi Yuan), was mostly destroyed in 1860 by the Anglo-French expedition. In 1887, the Empress Dowager Ci Xi reconstructed the garden with the money which should have been used for naval development. The rebuilding took eight years to complete and the new compound came to be called Yi He Yuan (Garden of Harmonious Unity), which is better known to the West as the Summer Palace.

The Summer Palace is 3.4 square kilometers in area, comprising the Kun Ming Lake and the Longevity Hill. The hilly area covers one fifth of the whole complex and reaches 60 meters in height. Functionally, the garden consists of three regions, one for handling state affairs, one for residences and one for pleasure.

The administrative region stretches from the East Palace Gate through to Benevolence Longevity Hall (Ren Shou Dian). At the back of Benevolence Longevity Hall are the three large quadrangular compounds of Jade Ripple Hall, Yi Yun House and Happiness Longevity Hall (Le Shou Tang), which were the living quarters of Emperor Guan Xu and the Empress Dowager Ci Xi. To the north of Benevolence Longevity Hall is Peaceful Garden (De He Yuan) in which the royal family watched operas.

The essence of the whole complex lies in the pleasance which comprises the front and back sides of the hill and Kun Ming Lake. Centered on the front side of the hill the Shining Cloud Jade Roofed Archway (Yunhui Yuyu Paifang) on the lake shore initiates an axis running north through the Cloud-dispelling Gate (Pai Yun Men), Cloud-dispelling Hall, Moral Glory Hall, Buddhist Fragrance Pavilion and the Temple of the Sea of Widsom. Rising along the slope in tiers, these buildings of yellow glazed roofs form the spine of the garden. The Zhuan Lun Zang Temple on the east side of this axis is set in juxtaposition to the Bronze Pavilion on the west to produce a sense of symmetry. Sprawling between the foothill and Kun Ming Lake, a 728 meter long walkway connects the east and west parts of the pleasance.

The main attraction of the back side of the hill lies in its serenity and archaic flavor. A clear stream flows from the Seaweed Bridge in the west, twisting and bending with the landscape before it reaches the Garden of Harmonious Interests (Xie Qu Yuan) in the east. Scattered over the landscape are remnant structures of Clear Ripple Garden, such as the Pine Hall south of North Palace Gate, Sumeru World, and the Four Great Realms (Sida Buzhou). Suzhou Street near the back lake is also a remnant of the 1860 destruction.

Along the eastern walkway, Appreciating the Spirit of Spring Pavilion (Zhi Chun Ting), God of Literature Hall (Wen Chang Ge), and the octagonal Extensive Pavilion (Guo Ru Ting) offer places to enjoy the lake scene. Towering over South Lake Island, the largest, Dragon King Temple, is connected to the shore by a seventeen arch bridge of 150 meters. On the pillars of the bridge balustrades are formed lifelike stone lions. Exquistely carved, each of the five hundred odd lions has its own distinctive posture.

The western walkway, constructed in Qian Long times, is modelled on the Su Causeway of West Lake. Its six bridges in different styles are also imitations of the bridges of the Su Causeway. The longest and most beautiful bridge among the six is called Jade Belt. It was the path for Emperor Qian Long when he traveled from Kun Ming Lake to Jade Spring Hill. On the pillars of its balustrades, stone cranes are so wonderfully carved that they look like the real bird.

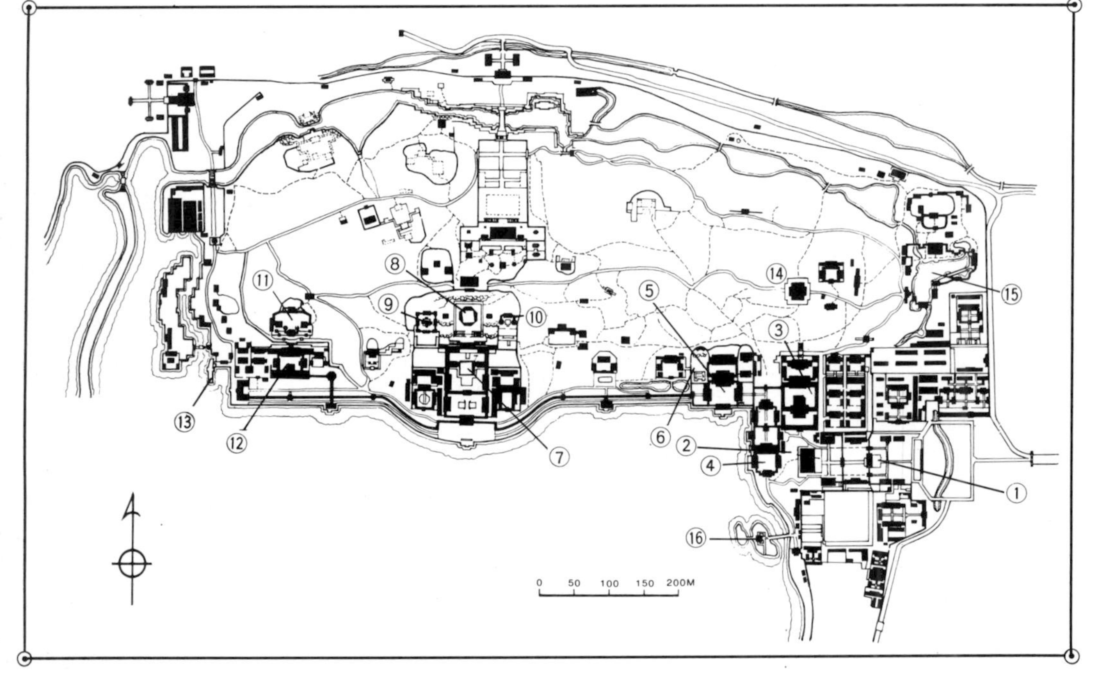

Summer Palace

1. *East Palace Gate*
2. *Benevolence Longevity Hall*
3. *Great Stage*
4. *Jade Ripple Hall*
5. *Happiness Longevity Hall*
6. *Yang Ren Feng, the small garden of Spreading the Spirit of Benevolence*
7. *Cloud-dispelling Hall*
8. *Buddhist Fragrance Pavilion*
9. *Bronze Pavilion*
10. *Zhuan Lun Zang Temple*
11. *Roving in Painting*
12. *Listening to Orioles Pavilion*
13. *stone boat*
14. *Jing Fu Pavilion*
15. *Garden of Harmonious Interest*
16. *Appreciating the Spirit of Spring Pavilion*

14

14. Seventeen Arch Bridge. 150 meters long, 8 meters wide, it is the longest stone bridge in classical Chinese gardens.

16

17

18

15. Kun Ming Lake and Longevity Hill at dawn
16. A view of Buddhist Fragrance Pavilion from Cloud-dispelling Hall
17. Shining Cloud Jade Roofed Archway
18. Kun Ming Lake

19

20

21

19. Panoramic view of Bronze Pavilion. Built entirely of bronze, it weighs 207 tons and was the praying hall of Qing emperors.

20. Roving in Painting, one of the main structures in west Longevity Hill

21. The octagonal seven-storied Duobao Glazed Pagoda

22

22. The gate tower of Crimson Wall Amidst Rosy Cloud

23. The long walkway, 728 meters long and highlighted by 4 pavilions and 14,000 color pictures of ***sushi*** *style. It is the longest walkway in classical Chinese gardens.*

德音汪濊

24

25

24. Bronze incense burner in front of the Hall of Benevolence and Longevity

*25. A **sushi** style color painting. Its theme emphasizes on landscape, flower and bird and figure and genre, **sushi** style color painting marks one of the most important features of Chinese imperial gardens.*

26

27

26. A view of Harmonious Interest Garden, a Qian Long era replica of Ji Chang Garden in Wuxi district.

27. Back part of the Kun Ming Lake

28

28. Understanding-the-Fish Bridge in Harmonious Interest Garden. The name is drawn from the discourse between the ancient philosopher Zhuang Zi and his friend Hui Shi who engaged in a sophist argument over whether one could understand the feeling of a fish.

29. Mirror Bridge, one of the six bridges at the West Causeway

Imperial Summer Resort

The largest imperial garden existing in China, the Chengde Imperial Summer Resort is embraced by mountains on four sides with the Wu Lie River running through its heart. Water from many hot springs flows into the Wu Lie River to make it ice free even in winter. This is a rare phenomenon in north China and the river is, therefore, also called the Re He — Hot River.

Chengde was chosen to be the site for the imperial summer resort since it was an important communication point and was only about 200 kilometers from the capital. The first construction of the compound began in 1703 when the Qing emperor Kang Xi ordered an imperial travel lodge to be built. The completed construction was called the Bishu Shanzhuang — Summer Resort. There were in total 36 *jing* (scenic spots) as designated by Emperor Kang Xi. During the reign of Qian Long, it was reconstructed and largely extended, with another 36 *jing* added to it and was named by the emperor. Since then, it has become the summer retreat of successive emperors as well as an important place for political meetings.

The garden in entirety covers an area of 5,600,000 square meters. Hilly regions constitute four-fifths of the total space while the remaining area is covered by plains and lakes. Rising and falling, the palace wall runs for ten kilometers. The resort can be divided functionally into two great regions: the administrative and residential region and the pleasance, the pleasance again subdivided into three geographical zones, namely the lake, the plain and the mountain.

The administrative and residential area lies in the southern portion of the resort. It comprises four groups of structures, all on a north-south alignment. In the west is the main palace complex. After entering the front gate, one reaches Nanmu Hall and Si Zhi Study which leads on to the royal sleeping chamber. To the east of the main palace is another group of structures. With the typical Chinese name of Pine Crane Study (Song He Zhai), this was the reception hall for leaders of the minority nationalities and foreign diplomats. Today, only remnants of the studio are left. The Pine Wind Sweeping Over Ten Thousand Vales Garden (Wan He Song Feng) to the north of the studio is a petite court on a hill by the water. The group of structures includes a memorial hall and the Jian Shi Studio. Going north from here, one may come into the lake region. The East Palace lies to the east of the residential region.

The lake region in the pleasance is tremendous in scale though it is only two-thirds of its original size which has been reduced as a result of sedimentation. The vast lake surface is cut into spaces of different sizes and shapes by islands, bridges and causeways, forming minor "lakes" such as the Ru Yi (S-shaped Jade) Lake, Clear Lake as well as Mirror and Silver lakes. Spreading around the vast lake are three clusters of landscape scenes. The middle cluster starts from the causeway of Zhi Jing Yun Ti (Heavenly Herb and Cloud Causeway) which links the garden court of Pine Wind Sweeping Over Ten Thousand Vales in the residential region with the built structures of Murmuring Stream in Moonlight (Yue Se Jiang Sheng), Ru Yi Island and Mist Rain Mansion in the lake region. The east cluster of scenes comprises the Lake Center Pavilions adjoining the East Palace, the Lion Grove within Literary Garden, Qing Shu Villa, Cheng De Hall, Flower Goddess Temple, Golden Mount and the Re He (Hot River). In the west, the Cloud Peak Gate (Yun Xiu Men) of the main palace serves as the dividing point between the administrative and residential region and the garden scenes in the lake area. Starting from here, the Fragrant Court Dwelling, Pavilion of the Streamside Fragrant Islet, Fragrant Villa, Mellifluous Pavilion (Ting Bao Ting), Meandering Stream Amidst Lotus Fragrance and Shore to the Sea of Literature (Wen Jin) Pavilion form the western scenic area.

Of the above scenic spots, some are worth special attention. The Zhi Jing Yun Ti causeway is modelled after the Su Causeway of the West Lake. The three pavilions called the Lake Center standing on the sluice dam are spots ideal for a clear glimpse of the surrounding scenery. Situated on the island north of the Lake Center Pavilions, Murmuring Stream in the Moonlight was the study area for the emperor in retreat. It is composed of a group of structures, the main ones being the Tranquil Villa and Bright Heart Hall. On the *ru yi* (an S-shaped ornamental object, usually made of jade, formerly a symbol of good luck) shaped Ru Yi Island are the elegant garden court of Golden Lotus Reflecting the Sun and a square pavilion called the Site for Viewing the Lotus. North of the Ru Yi Island is Green Lotus Islet. Mist Rain Mansion on the islet is a replica of the building of the same name at South Lake in Jia Xing district. It is the focal point of the lake scenes in the middle part. To the east of Ru Yi Island is Golden Mount. Set together with a group of huge rockeries, the structures on the mount model those on Golden Mount Temple in Zhenjiang district. The most important structure is the Golden Mount Pavilion which is also known as Heavenly Emperor's Pavilion.

Sprawling north of the lake area is the plain region. In the northeast is the Ten Thousand Tree Garden where pines, elms and trees of many kinds grow luxuriantly. The ancient structures which were built here no longer exist. To the west of the garden is the spacious Horses Testing Ground (Shima Dai).

The mountain region occupies the northwest part of the Summer Resort. Spreading over this region are rare shaped precipices and valleys such as Pine Cloud Canyon, Pear Tree Gorge, Pine Grove Vale, Hazel Peak and West Valley which all run from northwest to southeast. Originally there were many scenic spots and monasteries such as the Pear Blossom Accompanied by the Moon (Lihua Ban Yue) and the Zhu Yuan Temple. However, these fell into ruins due to lack of repair during the late Qing period. The Pavilion of Accumulated Snow Covering South Mountain, the Scenic Clouds and Hills Pavilion and the Pavilion of the Sunset at Hammer-shaped Peak are the only surviving structures besides a stone archway and two stone tablets.

Spreading over vast areas to the east and north of the Summer Resort were twelve temples which ran from south to north along the east coast of Wu Lie River and the north coast of Lion Ditch (Shizi Gou). Of these, only seven survive. These include such temples as the Great Benevolence (Pu Ren), Universal Joy (Pu Le), Long Consolidation (An Yuan), Universal Peace (Pu Ning), Sumeru Fortune and Longevity, Putuo Zongcheng and that of the Mañsuri Statue. Collectively, they are known to the world as the Wai Ba Temples.

30

30. Mist Rain Mansion, a replica of the building of the same name in South Lake, Jia Xing

31

32

33

31. The zigzag bridge leading to Mist Rain Mansion
32. Golden Mount Pavilion
33. Scenic Clouds and Hills Pavilion

34

35

36

34. The long causeway stretching across the lake
35. Lake Center Pavilions with reflections
36. North shore of Limpid Lake with the Lakeside Pavilion in the background
37. Pavilion of Accumulated Snow Covering the South Mountain (Nanshan Jixue Ting) after a snowfall

38

39

40

41

42

38. Heavenly Herb Path and Cloud Causeway at dawn
39. Hammered-shaped Peak at sunrise
40. Distant view of the Pagoda of Yongyou Temple
41. The beautiful lake and mountain
42. Autumn scene in the mountain region

Magnificent Clear Lake

Twenty-five kilometers away from Xi'an (formerly Chang'an) in Lintong, Shaanxi Province, is Mount Li (Li Shan). On its north side is the Magnificent Clear Lake (Hua Qing Chi), a lake one frequently comes across in classical Chinese literary works.

Originally known as the Hot Spring Palace (Tangquan Gong), it was first built by the great Tang emperor Tai Zong. During the reign of Xuan Zong, it was expanded and renamed Magnificent Clear Palace (Hua Qing Gong). Described in the records as a stupendous complex comprising halls, pavilions, a hot water well, and a lake, it was here that the famous romance between Emperor Xuan Zong and his concubine Yang Guifei took place. The "Song of Everlasting Sorrow (Chang Hen Ge)" by the celebrated Tang poet Bai Juyi depicts this story so successfully that the song itself has become a well-known literary piece and the site a name full of literary associations. The palace was destroyed in the Rebellion of An Lushan and Shi Siming and converted into a monastery during the Five Dynasties period. The present buildings are reconstructions dating from the Qing Dynasty.

Today Magnificent Clear Lake is a small scale garden compound. The garden's structures center around a lotus filled lake fed by spring water flowing down from Mount Li in the background. Rising and falling according to the topography, the built structures are made accessible to one another by mountain paths and steps.

The main entrance of the garden, known as Lakeview Mansion, is in the north. A two-storied structure, its upper floor is an open hall *(ge)* while the lower story comprises a gate with three openings. The east and west sides of the mansion are connected to each other by a passageway and a gallery. From the mansion, a panoramic view of the whole garden is in sight.

At the center is a lake bedecked with lotuses. To its west are the Boat Pavilion, Flying Rosy Cloud Pavilion and the Yang Guifei Pool. Further west on a slope are such buildings as the Five Bay Hall and the Yang Hall. On the slope east of the lake the Flag Pavilion, Tablet Pavilion, Rainbow Bridge and Pavilion for Viewing the River make up the principal structures. The Rainbow Bridge leads through Kai Yang Gate to the former East Garden of Tang times where remnants of Tang structures such as the Delightful Spring Pavilion, Mansion for Viewing Phoenixes, Hall of Cock Fighting and the Jiao Garden can be found. Going east up the hill along a stone path, one reaches the Zhuo Chiang Ting, or Pavilion Where Chiang Kai-shek Was Captured (in the 1936 Xi'an Incident). Climbing upwards, the Lao Jun Temple is visible amidst the surrounding greenery. At the top of Mount Li is a structure said to be the Beacon Tower (Fenghuo Tai) where Emperor You of the Western Zhou Dynasty (11th century B.C. to 771 B.C.) greatly alarmed all his feudal lords by lighting up a beacon fire, simply in order to amuse his concubine Bao Si.

In 1957 a garden in the Tang style was added to the compound. Situated west of the square at the north gate, all buildings in the garden are named after similar Tang structures. Even the name of the garden — Garden of Nine Dragon Lake — is the same as the lake where Emperor Xuan Zong bathed.

43

43. Lakeview Mansion, main entrance to Magnificent Clear Lake with Mount Li in the backdrop.

44

45

44. Magnificent Clear Lake in the morning mist
45. Source of the hot spring
46. Rainbow Bridge

Private Gardens

Ke Garden (Beijing)

Ke Garden is situated in the northeast corner of the Forbidden City in Maor Lane. The residence of the royal prince Rong Yuan, it was first built during the years of Emperor Xian Feng of the Qing. The garden proper is to the east of the living quarters. The shape of the garden is elongated with a north-south length of 100 meters and a east-west width of 26 meters. It is one of the best preserved traditional gardens.

This small garden is formed by two sections, north and south. In the east is a long gallery which connects the two parts. The main attraction of the garden is in its architecture, with the landscape complementing the scene. The main structures align along a central axis while the buildings on the two sides are so arranged as to break the rigid balance of ordinary living compounds.

The north court is smaller, with buildings on four sides. The main structure, with a formal *xieshan* roof (half-hipped, half-gabled roof with decorative ridges), is in the north. In the east, a two-storied pavilion stands on a two meter high terrace. The pavilion is accessible by galleries from both the north and south. To the south of this storied pavilion is a smaller pavilion, square in shape. The main entrance of the court is in the west, and a gallery joins it with the northern structures.

The larger south court is the scenic spot of the whole compound. The main structure is again in the north, with its roof in the less formal *juanpeng* style (simple half-hipped, half-gabled roof). In the west is a gallery dotted with pavilions; an artificial hill functions as a screen for the south entrance. The hill is three meters high, and on its top is erected a small hexagonal pavilion, which obviously lengthens its apparent height. A cave can be found on each of the east and west hillsides, and on the north face is a naturally shaped pond. The northern part of the hill is created with the Fangshan stone with its reins running vertically while the southern part is constructed of grey-green *qingshi* rock with horizontal veins. The combination of rocks is peculiar to this hill.

The interior design of the garden also has its unique features, with patterns of pine, bamboo and plum blossom adopted for all its wood carvings.

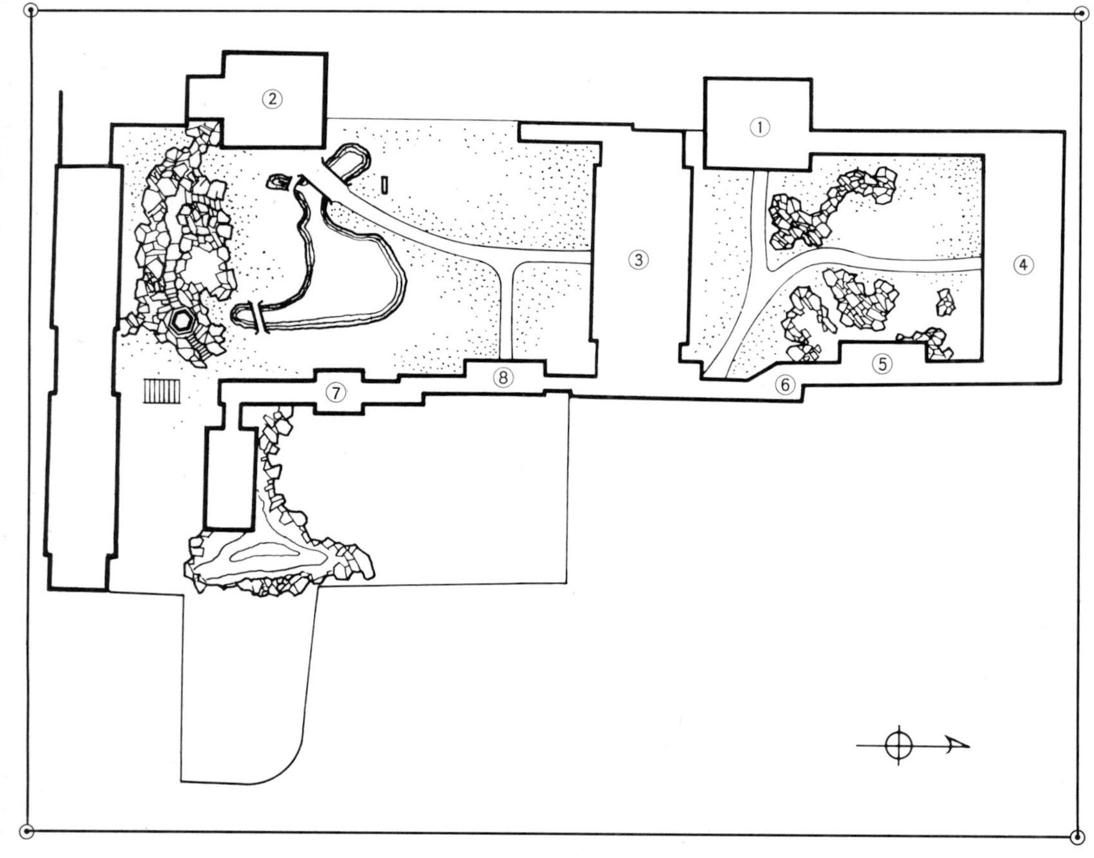

Ke Garden
1. *north entrance*
2. *south entrance*
3. *middle hall*
4. *north main hall*
5. *two-storied pavilion*
6. *square pavilion*
7. *hexagonal pavilion*
8. *side hall*

47

47. The pleasant, tranquil Ke Garden

48

49

50

48. Rockeries at the north garden court
49. The square pavilion and gallery
50. Pavilion and corridor on the east side
51. A sundial, stone table and seats

Liu Yong's Garden

Liu Yong was a Grand Secretary serving in the Qing court during the Qian Long period. Alias Liu Shi'an, he was a famous calligrapher, and within his residence he built the small landscape garden which bears his name.

Liu Yong's residence is found in the Lishi Hutong (Lishi Lane) at East City, Beijing. Measuring 40 meters from east to west and 35 meters north to south, the garden boasts an excellent view of natural landscape. In the northeast is a five meter high earth mount studded with rocks which appears to be a range of great mountains. At the foot, the banks of a pond bend in the shade of trees and flowers grow luxuriantly.

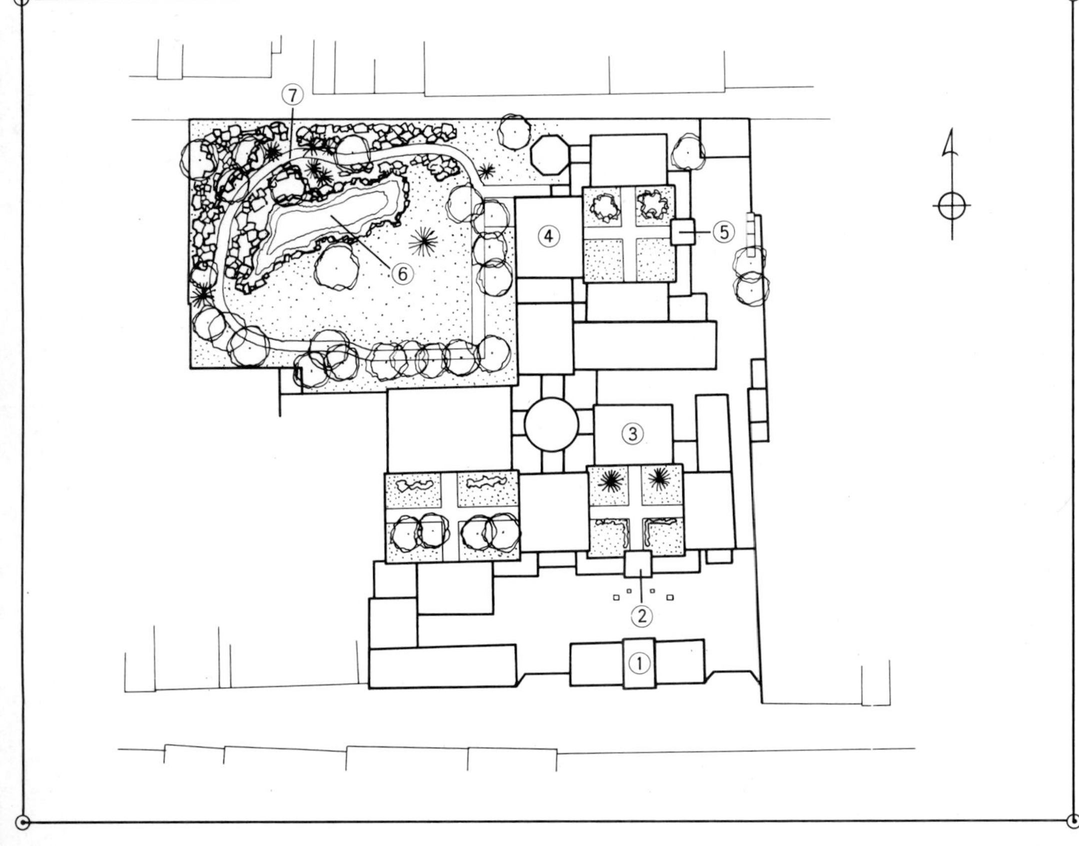

Liu Yong's Garden
1. *main gate*
2. ***chui hua men*** *— the second gate*
3. *main hall*
4. *main chamber of the back court*
5. ***chui hua men*** *of the back court*
6. *pool*
7. *rockeries*

53

52. Large traditional living compounds in the north usually have a second gate called *chui hua men. Shown here is the chui hua men of Liu Yong's Garden.*

53. The garden with rocks scattered in a world of refreshing greenery

54

55

54. A small building with a ***xieshan*** *(half-hipped, half-gabled) style roof. It is connected to the side wall of the eastern living quarters.*

55. Detail of the brick carvings on the wall of the building

Zhan Garden

Zhan Garden was said to be the residence of Xu Da , a distinguished general who helped the first Ming emperor found the dynasty. In the early Qing dynasty, it was changed to the garden of the provincial governor. Emperor Qian Long visited here twice when he traveled south, and even wrote the inscription on the lintel tablet hanging over the front entrance gate, making it instantly well-known throughout the country. During the Taiping Revolution, it had once been the residence of the East Prince Yang Xiuqing and that of the Vice Premier Lai Hanying. It was destroyed later in war and restored during the time of emperors Tong Zhi and Guang Xu of the Qing. After 1949 it was completely rennovated, with a miniature mountain in the south constructed.

Zhan Garden is located at Zhan Garden Road. The building to its east has been made the Memorial Hall of the Taiping Revolution. From north to south, the garden measures 120 meters long while it stretches 40 meters from east to west, forming a long narrow shape.

In the center towards the south the main structure, Tranquility Hall (Jing Miao Hall), divides the garden into two parts, each with a pond and a miniature mountain. In the Tranquility Hall, one can enjoy the scenes from both parts. To the east there is a high wall; going along with the wall all the way from north to south is a long verandah highlighted by two pavilions. To the west is an earthen mount with a stone path sprawling in the midst of bamboo groves. Below the mount is an elongated lake which joins the south pond with the one in the north. The main entrance to the garden is at the south. After entry, a view of the rockery of Immortal's Peak can be seen through the lattice window. This rockery is said to be a tribute to the Song emperor Hui Zong.

The garden is famed for its miniature mountains. The one in the north is left from the old days. On the side of the mountain is a small path leading up and through the whole creation, passing through caves and crevices. Spanning over the pond south of the mountain is a stone bridge with three turns. Stretching from a mass of rocks rising one higher than another, it reaches out to the other side of the pond which fills the whole place with natural rustic charm. The miniature mountain in the south part was constructed in the early 1960s. Rising and falling, the mountain range sprawls left and right while on the top rockeries of rare shapes stand in magnificence. At the foothill, crevices forming images of stalactites and stalagmites are washed by water flowing down from the heights to join the pond. With its rare formations, this miniature mountain is considered one of the best of its kind.

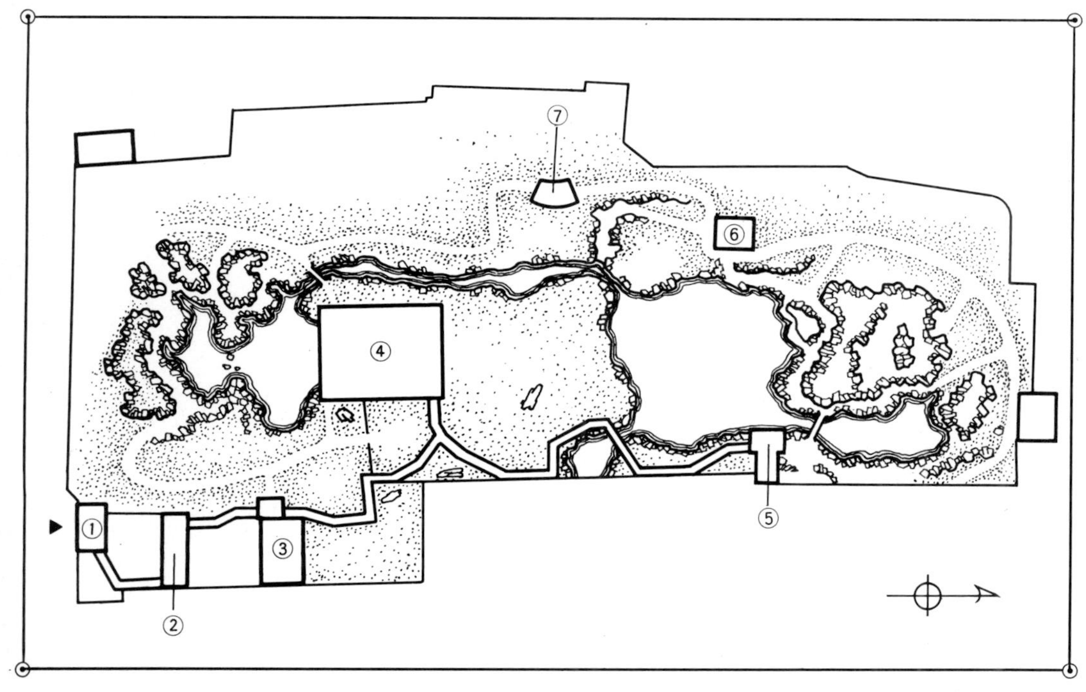

Zhan Garden
1. *entrance*
2. *small hall*
3. *Flower Basket Hall*
4. *Tranquility Hall*
5. *waterside pavilion*
6. *square pavilion*
7. *fan-shaped pavilion*

56

56. *The dainty pavilion standing by the pond at the east entrance*

57

57. The entrance gate. With such a plain appearance that it looks like a door for ordinary living quarters. Passing the gate and looking through the lattice window, one comes across the Immortal's Peak of Taihu eroded limestone.

58. Tranquility Hall and the pond out onto which the hall extends

58

59

59. A forked gallery partitioning the garden scene and adding to its attractions

60. Trellis over a lawn

60

Ge Garden

Ge Garden is situated at Dong Mei Street in Xin Cheng, Yangzhou. Built in the Jia Qing period of the Qing Dynasty by a salt merchant, Huang Zhiyun, it was originally called the Shou Zhi Garden. When Huang Yingtai became the new owner, bamboo trees, a symbol of integrity to the Chinese, were widely planted. This garden of bamboos came to be called ''Ge'' since the Chinese character for ''ge'' (个) makes up half of the character for bamboo (竹). By calling it ''Ge'', it is apparent that the owner was making an association to the famous line ''A gentleman is not to live without bamboo.''

Rectangular in plan, the garden stretches from east to west, with the entrance in the south. After entering, one comes to the Osmanthus Hall (Gui Hua Ting) near the center. Spacious and open on four sides, this is the main building of the garden. To the north of the hall is a pond surrounded by rockeries, and on the east bank stands a small pavilion. Running over the pond is a stone bridge which stretches north to join a seven bay building. From the top of the building, an overall view of the garden is in sight. The building is connected by a long gallery with miniature mountains in the east and west.

With compositions of four miniature mountains, Ge Garden is noted for being very representative of Yangzhou traditional gardens. The mountains are constructed of different kinds of rocks, with their formations, colors and textures all different from each other. Known commonly as ''the miniature mountains of four seasons'', they embody different artistic conceptions.

At the entrance in the south the Spring Mountain stands amidst a grove of bamboo and stone bamboo shoots, making up a spring scene. The Summer Mountain is in the western part of the garden. Constructed of *hushi* eroded limestone, this stack of rocks is full of cavities, jagged and precipitous, with rocks folding one on top of another. At the foot of the mountain, the entrance of a cave is half submerged in a pond from which a stone path extends into its mouth. The depth of the cave seems unfathomable. Inside, a stone path leads up through a few turns to the top of the mountain. In the east part of the garden, the Autumn Mountain constitutes another scene. Created out of yellow *huangshi* granite, it is complete with peaks, precipices, gorges and winding paths. The crevices and cliffs are cut with so high a skill that they appear to be formed by natural corrosion. In the southeast corner of the garden, the Winter Mountain stands in front of the Moon Breeze Pavilion (Touyue Loufeng Xuan). A rockery of white *xuanshi* stone, it has the appearance of a real mountain in cold winter.

In the center of the garden is a hall open on four sides. From inside the hall one can leisurely enjoy the surrounding scenes. In the rear of the hall, a two-storied hexagonal pavilion offers an overall view of the garden.

61

61. Entrance
62. Summer Mountain. Piled up entirely of ***hushi*** *eroded limestone and forming a harmonious unity with the pond, it is a successful piece of art.*

62

Ji Chang Garden

Ji Chang Garden is one of the most well-known gardens south of the Yangtze River. Built in the Zheng De era of the Ming Dynasty, it was owned by a certain Qin family, with an original name of ''Fenggu Xingwo (Phoenix Abode).'' At the beginning of the reign of Emperor Kang Xi of Qing, Zhang Shi, newphew of the famous craftsman Zhang Nanyuan, built a miniature mountain in the garden, making it more splendid than ever. The Qing emperors Kang Xi and Qian Long, when they came south, both visited this garden. Emperor Qian Long especially relished it, and when back in Beijing, he ordered the construction of the Xie Qu Garden in the Summer Palace, to be modelled on the Ji Chang.

Ji Chang Garden runs north-south in a rectangular shape, with the higher western part sloping gently down to the east. In the west stands Mount Wei and in the south, Mount Xi. Flowing down Mount Wei are many natural streams, which at ground level form the Lake of Embroidery Ripples.

Centered around the Embroidery Ripple Lake, the architecture of the garden sprawls in all directions. On the east bank stands a group of pavilions and corridors with the Yu Pan Pavilion and Zhi Yu Balustrade stretching in a zigzag into the water, offering a good place to enjoy the scene in the east. To the north of the lake is the Jia Shu Hall which has been turned into a teahouse. Looking south from the hall, the distant view of the Mount Xi Pagoda with its reflection in the water will come in sight. In the past, there were still more structures in the north and east of the garden which, however, have been destroyed.

In the layout of the buildings in the north and south, the traditional garden-making skill of ''borrowing views'' is utilized. To the lake's west is a miniature mountain decorated with trees and *huangshi* granite. With Mount Wei as its backdrop, the miniature is so arranged that it appears to be a range of the actual mountain. In such a way, the artificial merges with the natural. The Eight Tune Ravine, constructed entirely with *huangshi,* is a noted feature. Murmuring down the ravine, a little stream adds to the beauty of the rockery.

From the west bank of the Embroidery Ripple Lake, a long strip of rock, the He Bu Tan, stretches out to the center. Together with Zhi Yu Balustrade projecting from the other side, the He Bu Tan gives the lake the shape of a bottle gourd. North of the lake is the Seven Star Bridge connecting the east and west shores. Viewed either from the north or the south, scene after scene of the lake seems to extend into the far, far distance.

63

63. A scene from Embroidery Ripple Lake, ''borrowing'' the view of Mount Xi in the distance.

64

65

64. *The Zhi Yu Balustrade and the rock strip of He Bu Tan stretching out into Embroidery Ripple Lake*
65. *Stone table and seats in Yu Pan Pavilion. Here the Qing emperor Qian Long once played chess with a monk.*

66

67

66. *Eight Tune Ravine. Gurgling down the rocks, it makes visitors feel as if they were wandering on a remote mountain.*
67. *The miniature mountain and stream that merge with Mount Wei*

Zhuo Zheng Garden

Representative of a traditional Suzhou garden, Zhuo Zheng Garden, or Garden of the Unsuccessful Politician, is located at the Northeast Street of Lou Men, Suzhou. It was built in the Jia Jing period of the Ming Dynasty by Wang Xianchen, Censor of the Throne. The name comes from a line in the "Xian Ju (An Idle Life)" rhyme-prose composed by the famous scholar-official Pan Yue of the Jin Dynasty. Once when Pan was disappointed in his political life, he retired to live in a farmhouse and led an idle life planting trees and growing vegetables. In the "Xian Ju" rhyme-pose he writes "This *is* the way of ruling for an unsuccessful politician." The garden frequently changed its owners and with each new owner, much reconstruction was done. During the time of the Taiping Heavenly Kingdom, it served as the residence of the Loyal Prince, Li Xiucheng.

The whole garden complex is composed of three parts, with the Garden of the Unsuccessful Politician at the center, flanked by the Affiliated Garden (Bu Yuan) to the west and the Hermit's Farmhouse (Gui Tianyuan Ju) to the east.

The Garden of the Unsuccessful Politician is the essence of the complex. With a lake as the center of the whole layout, the main structures all stand along the shore. Carved into portions of different shapes by bridges and islets, the lake offers a rich variation of views. The main building is the Distant Fragrance Hall (Yuan Xiang Hall), from which one can leisurely enjoy the surrounding scenery. To the west of the hall, the Leaning Jade Pavilion (Yi Yu Xuan), Fragrant Island, Jade Wave Hall, True Spirit Pavilion (De Zhen Ting), Little Surging Wave Pavilion, Small Rainbow Roofed Bridge, each with a distinctive style and form, compose a rich scene. Looking north from the Distant Fragrance Hall, a vast surface of water with a mountain in its background comes in sight. On the mountain perches the Pavilion of Fragrant Snow and Azure Sky (Xuexiang Yunwei Ting). Running from the east to the south of the Distant Fragrance Hall is a miniature mountain constructed with earth and rock, and on a mountain to the east is the Embroidery Pavilion (Xiu Yi Ting). To the south of the pavilion is the Loquat Garden (Pi Pa Yuan). The garden, an area enclosed by a cloud wall, is paved with colorful pebblestones which form beautiful patterns. In the cloud wall is a moon gate which makes a frame for the Pavilion of Fragrant Snow and Azure Sky.

Passing through the Pavilion Leading to a New World (Bieyou Dongtian) is the Affiliated Garden. To the west, the organizational plan again uses a lake as the center. The main built structure is the 36 Mandarin Ducks Hall (Sanshiliu Yuanyang Guan) to the south of the lake. To the north is the miniature mountain with a pavilion on its peak. In the southwestern corner is the Pagoda Shadow Pavilion (Ta Ying Ting). Together with a brooklet and a water corridor, it constitutes a most perfect landscape garden creation.

From the Pavilion of Haitang Flowers Blossoming in Spring (Haitang Chunwu), one can pass on to the eastern garden, which was the old site of the Hermit's Farmhouse (Gui Tianyuan Ju). After the establishment of the People's Republic, the government had the eastern garden extended. With a vast lawn and a square grove of pine trees, the garden combines the features of both the traditional and the modern.

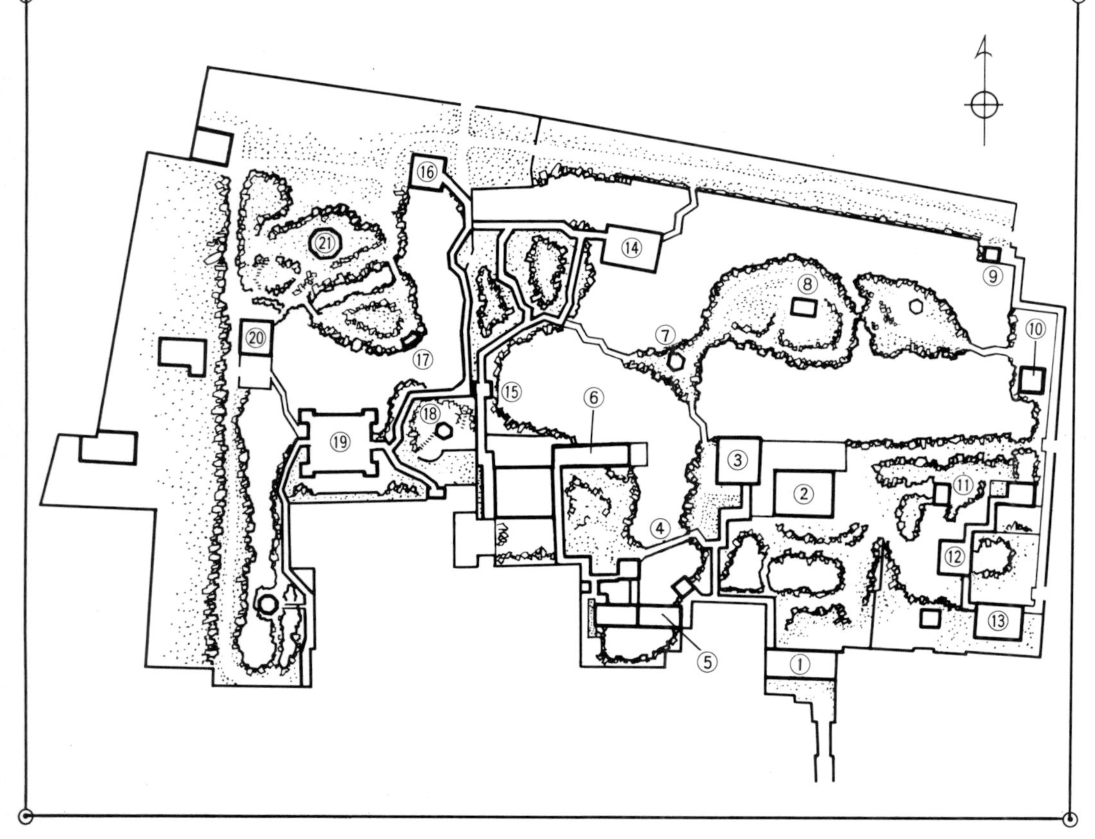

Zhuo Zheng Garden

1. *entrance*
2. *Distant Fragrance Hall*
3. *Leaning Jade Pavilion*
4. *Small Rainbow Roofed Bridge*
5. *Little Surging Wave Pavilion*
6. *Fragrant Island*
7. *Pavilion of Lotus Wind Blowing from All Sides*
8. *Pavilion of Fragrant Snow and Azure Sky*
9. *Green Ripple Pavilion*
10. *Secluded House Amidst Parasol and Bamboo*
11. *Embroidery Pavilion*
12. *Dainty Hall*
13. *Listening to the Rain Pavilion*
14. *Mountain View Mansion*
15. *Pavilion Leading to a New World*
16. *Reflection Pavilion*
17. *Pavilion for Sitting Together With a Friend*
18. *the hexagonal Yi Yu Pavilion*
19. *36 Mandarin Ducks Hall*
20. *Liu Ting Pavilion*
21. *Floating Green Pavilion*

68

68. Distant Fragrance Hall and Leaning Jade Pavilion on the south shore of the lake. Distant Fragrance is the main structure in Zhuo Zhen Garden. Facing the Snowy Cloudy Pavilion perching on an islet, it offers a sweeping view and is an ideal place to enjoy the surrounding scenery. (photography by Feng Yunqing)

69

70

71

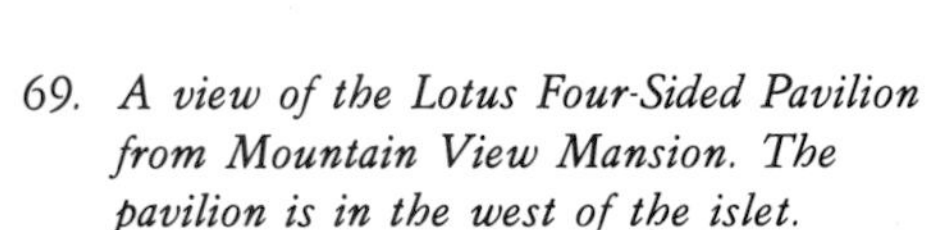

69. A view of the Lotus Four-Sided Pavilion from Mountain View Mansion. The pavilion is in the west of the islet.
70. Lingshui Long Gallery in the east of Affiliated Garden and Yi Yu Pavilion in the southeast, forming a beautiful profile.
71. Looking through the slightly arched Small Rainbow Bridge, one feels the view stretching far into the distance.

73

74

72. *Green Ripple Pavilion in the northeast of the Zhuo Zhen Garden*
73. *Lake in the Affiliated Garden. With piled rocks stretching out into the water with trees and wild grass growing around, the illusion of a natural lake is created.*
74. *The cave gates of the Wu Zhu Yiuju Pavilion, making up interesting frames for the surrounding scenes.*

Liu Garden

Liu Garden (Lingering Garden) is situated outside the Chong Men. One of the largest gardens in Suzhou, it was built during the reign of Emperor Wan Li of the Ming Dynasty by Xu Shitai who named it Dong Yuan or East Garden. During the Jia Qing period of the Qing Dynasty, Liu Shu rebuilt it and changed its name to Cold Green Villa (Han Bi Shan Zhuang). Emperor Guang Xu refurbished it again and renamed it Liu Garden.

Liu Garden is divided into four parts. In the middle is the site of the Cold Green Villa which is the chief beauty spot in the garden compound. The north, east and west parts were renovated during the Guang Xu era.

At the site of the Cold Green Villa, built structures occupy most of the east part, encompassing Meandering Stream Mansion, Five Peak Hall for the Immortals (or Nanmu Hall), Crane Nest (He Suo), Bowing Peak (Yifeng) Pavilion and a study called Huanwo Dushuchu. Varying in size, these buildings stand together to make an interesting pattern, with galleries turning and zigzagging to connect them. To the west of the villa site a miniature mountain is silhouetted against a lake. To the south of the lake are Greeny House (Han Bi Shan Fang) and Bright Clear Mansion (Ming Se Lou), which make up the most important scene in the site. Turning eastwards, one will pass the Green Shade Building (Lü Yin) and the Hall of Crisscrossing Ancient Tree Branches (Gumu Jiaoke) which are connected by a gallery to the Meandering Stream Bridge in the east. To the north of the lake is a miniature mountain and a grove, in the midst of which the tips of several pavilions can dimly be seen. In the middle of the lake is the Islet of the Immortals, with a bridge connecting it to the east shore. To the west is another miniature mountain, on the peak of which stands the Fragrant Wood Pavilion. From the pavilion, a view of the whole garden can be had.

In the eastern part of the compound, the Hall for Hermits and the Respectful (Linquan Qishi Guan), Cloud Capped Terrace (Guan Yun Tai) and the Mansion of the Cloud Capped Terrace (Guan Tai Lou) cluster around a courtyard. In the courtyard artificial peaks form the main theme with small ponds dotting all around. The tight organization contrasts greatly with the spaciousness of the central garden. Among the peaks, the Cloud Capped Peak is about nine meters high. Gaunt, creased with chinks and punched with holes, it is the only one of its kind in Suzhou.

To the west is a hillock liberally planted with maple trees, scattered among which are tiny pavilions. Climbing this mount one can see Suzhou's famous Tiger Hill Pagoda.

The design of the Liu Garden is very rich and complex. It is finely constructed, its layout carefully planned. This garden is especially famous for its wonderful utilization of windows and openings as the frames for beautiful views both close and afar.

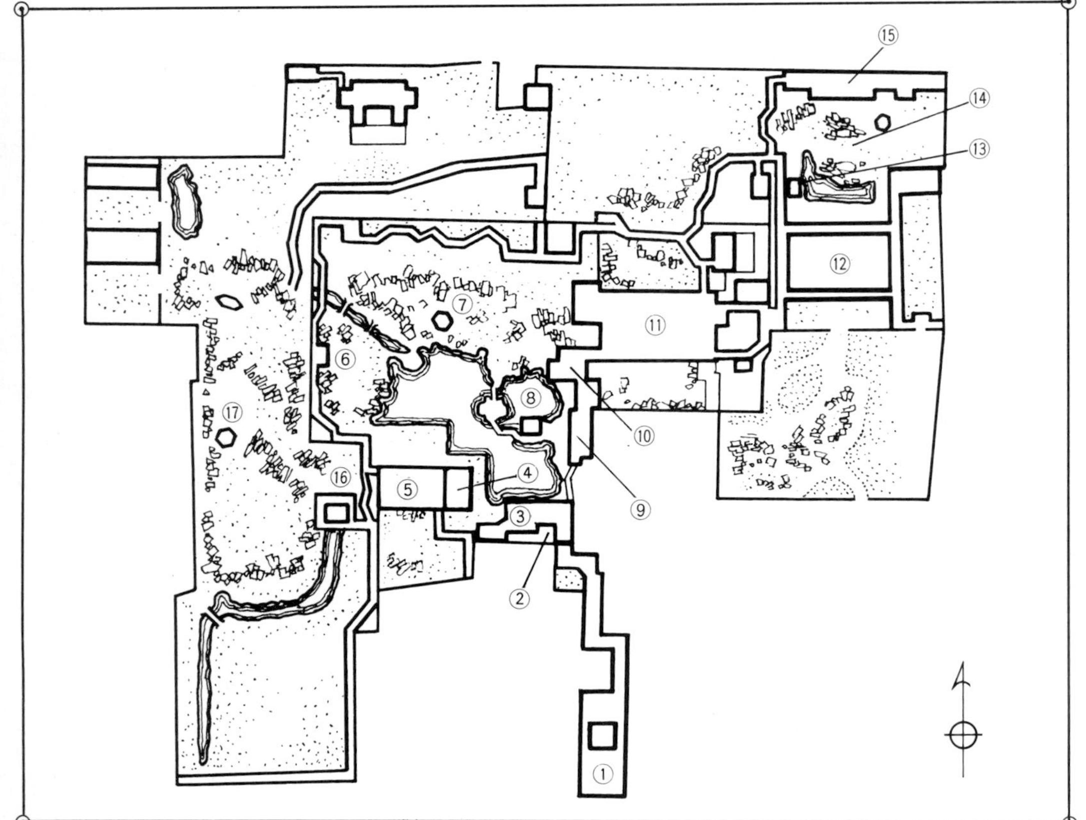

Liu Garden

1. *entrance*
2. *Hall of Crisscrossing Ancient Tree Branches*
3. *Green Shade Building*
4. *Bright Clear Mansion*
5. *Greeny House*
6. *Fragrant Wood Pavilion*
7. *Ke Pavilion*
8. *Hao Pu Pavilion*
9. *Meandering Stream Mansion*
10. *Waterside Hall of Fresh Breeze*
11. *Five Peak Hall for the Immortals*
12. *Hall for Hermits and the Respectful*
13. *Cloud Capped Terrace*
14. *Cloud Capped Peak*
15. *Mansion of the Cloud Capped Terrace*
16. *Lively Region*
17. *Pavilion for Whistling and Singing*

75

75. Liu Garden with its buildings, trees, rockeries and lake merging into one entity

77

78

79

76. *Courtyard of the Cloud Capped Peak, with its layout focused on the peak. Gaunt, creased with chinks and punched with holes, the peak is nine meters high and constructed of* ***hushi*** *Taihu eroded limestone.*
77. *Fresh Breeze Hall, Meandering Stream Mansion and Hao Pu Pavilion*
78. *A zigzag gallery*
79. *North shore of the lake with the Ke Pavilion perching on a miniature mountain in the background*

80

81

80. *A lattice window*

81. *Highly elaborate touch ground windows with wooden frames in the Nanmu Hall*

82

83

82. A path paved in floral design
83. An inside view of the Nanmu Hall

Wang Shi Garden

Wang Shi Garden, or Garden of the Master of the Fishing Nets, was originally the garden of the Song official Shi Zhengzhi and bore the name Thousand Scroll Hall. It was rebuilt during the reign of Emperor Qian Long and changed to its present name.

The whole compound is made up of a garden and living quarters. The garden is located in the west, with a lake serving as the central point of the layout. On the lake's shores, corridors, pavilions, stone bridges and rockeries compose a scene of rich attractions. Alongside the lake are picturesque grottos of yellow *huangshi* granite, in the creation of which techniques derived from Chinese painting were applied.

To the north of the lake are such buildings as the Pavilion for Viewing Pines and Enjoying Paintings and the Void Studio (Ji Xu Zhai). Standing tall and short, dense and sparse, these buildings compose a visually fascinating scene along the north shore. To the west is a quiet petite court with Late Spring Abode (Dian Chun Yi) as its main building. To the south are Small Hill Osmanthus Bush Pavilion, Pavilion of Clean Water for Cap-string Washing, Stick to Peace Mansion and Lute Chamber, comprising courtyards of quiet seclusion. The chief structure is the Small Osmanthus Bush Pavilion which is screened off from the lake by a big rockery.

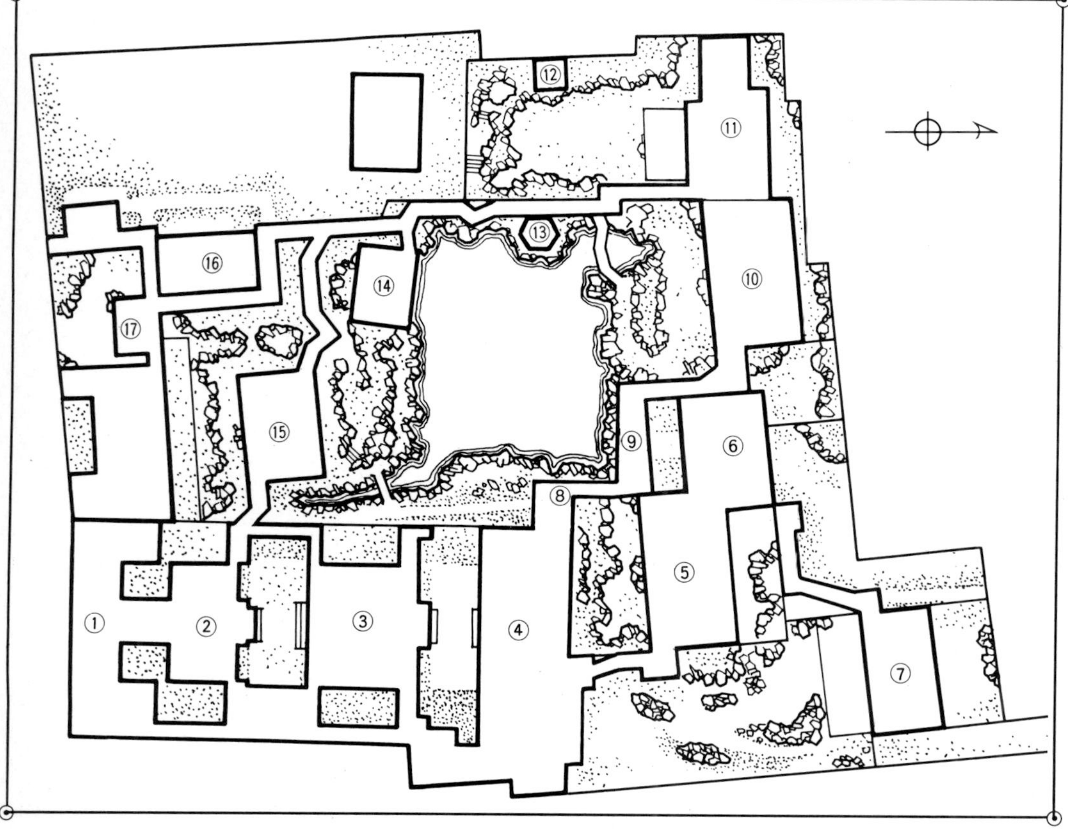

Wang Shi Garden

1. *entrance*
2. *chair hall*
3. *reception hall*
4. *Hall of Gathering Fragrance*
5. *Five Peak Studio*
6. *Void Studio*
7. *Cloud Ladder House*
8. *Duck Shooting Gallery*
9. *Pavilion of A Branch Beyond the Bamboo*
10. *Pavilion for Viewing Pines and Enjoying Paintings*
11. *Late Spring Abode*
12. *Cold Spring Pavilion*
13. *Moon Coming Wind Arriving Pavilion*
14. *Pavilion of Clean Water for Cap-string Washing*
15. *Small Hill Osmanthus Bush Pavilion*
16. *Stick to Peace Mansion*
17. *Lute Chamber*

84

85

86

84. A picturesque view framed in the gate of a plain wall. Full of poetic flavor, the view can be conceived as a three dimensional Chinese painting of ''a small bridge, riverlet and house''.

85. Courtyard of Late Spring Abode, a fine example of Suzhou minor courts.

86. The Zhuwaiyizhi (A Branch Beyond the Bamboo) Pavilion by the lakeside. The regularity of the pavilion makes an interesting contrast with the irregularity of the shoreline.

87

88

87. Carvings and inscriptions at the door of the main hall

88. Rockeries at the back of Xiaoshan Conggui Pavilion. Rising and falling along a narrow path, they form a rhythmic scene.

89. Scenes framed in the windows of Late Spring Abode (photograph by Feng Yunqing)

90. Stone balustrade and paved path in the courtyard of the Late Spring Abode

91. Duck Shooting Gallery and Zhuwaiyizhi Pavilion. The buildings are so arranged that the void and the solid are well juxtaposed.

89

90

Lion Grove Garden

Lion Grove Garden was first built in the Zhi Zheng period of the Yuan Dynasty. It was originally part of the Puti Zhengzong Temple. Inside the garden there are many rockeries in the shape of a lion *(shizi),* hence the name Lion Grove, or Shizi Lin in Chinese. The celebrated painter, Ni Zan, one of the four masters of the Yuan, captured the beauty of the garden in his famous Scroll of Lion Grove Garden, making the garden more renowned than ever. The Qing emperors Kang Xi and Qian Long visited the garden several times and they had a garden built modelled after it in the Imperial Summer Resort in Rehe (Jehol).

Carefully designed, the east part of the garden is decorated with many rockeries while the west part is covered by a vast body of water. The main structures are to the north, with the pavilions and halls all connected to one another by long galleries. Up and down, turning and twisting, these galleries are well-known for their unique format.

After entering by the gate in the southeast corner of the garden complex, one passes the Yan Yu Hall and Xiao Fang Hall (Small Square Hall). In the backyard of Xiao Fang Hall is a plum-blossom-shaped gate, and in the front of the gate are bamboo trees and rockeries, evoking a perfectly framed Chinese painting. To the north of the plum blossom gate is the Pavilion for Pointing to the Cypress which is the main structure of the whole garden. Looking south from the pavilion, one can see an expanse of rockeries with a forest of cypress trees standing high in their midst. To the southwest of the pavilion is Mountain View Mansion and Lotus Hall which, facing the lake, comprise a vantage point where one can admire the lotuses unobstructed. Further west is the Genuine Amusement Pavilion, Stone Boat and Faint Fragrance Dim Shadow Mansion (Anxiang Shuying Lou), all of which line the shore of the nearby lake. Turning south along the porch on the west, one comes to the Flying Waterfall Pavilion which is the highest spot in the garden. Under the pavilion is a *hushi* limestone rockery of three layers which drops steeply to join a brook at its foot. Further south are the Pavilion for Greeting the Plum Blossoms (Wen Mei Ting) and Double Fragrance Hall of the Immortals which is at the southwest corner of the garden. To its east, the Fan-Shaped Pavilion and the Pavilion of the Memorial Tablet of Wen Tianxiang (a loyal Song official) mark the southern border of the garden.

The specialities of Lion Grove Garden are its miniature mountains and peaks. The miniature mountain in front of Pointing to Cypress Pavilion has the most peculiar formation. Among its peaks, the Sunshine, Moon Rising, Black Jade and Sky Touching all have their own characteristics, with Lion Peak being the highest. Stone paths connecting the grottos and caves, which are located high and low over the mountain, form a labyrinth. The design of each cave and grotto is different and taken together they make up the famous Eighteen Scenes, with the Hall Sleeping on Clouds (Woyun Shi) situated in the middle. Constructed entirely with *hushi* eroded limestone, this miniature mountain looks grotesque and towering.

92

92. Lake Center and Genuine Amusement pavilions

93

94

95

93. The path on the west side of Pavilion for Pointing to the Cypress in Lion Grove Garden
94. The plum blossom shaped gate
95. Lotus Hall and Mountain View Mansion in the background of a lake. The rockeries in the lake make the latter appear deeper than it is.

Garden of the Surging Wave Pavilion

The Garden of Surging Wave Pavilion is the oldest of all Suzhou gardens, being built at the end of the Five Dynasties as the villa of Sun Chengyou. In the Northern Song Dynasty, the poet Su Shunqin built the Surging Wave Pavilion at the villa, and in the Southern Song the famous general Han Shizhong who fought the Nuzhen Tartars lived here. In the Ming Dynasty it became a temple. A large part of the garden today was reconstructed during the Qing Dynasty.

At the entrance are an archway with the garden's name inscribed on it and a stone bridge. Going east after passing the bridge one comes to the Pavilion Facing Water which is situated by the side of a lake to its north and faces a miniature mountain to its south. Moving on, one can enjoy the scenes inside and outside the garden through the lattice windows on the walls of a long double gallery. Further east is the Fishing Terrace, a pavilion by the shore of the lake. From the Fishing Terrace a gallery joins a path which leads to the main structure of the garden, the Surging Wave Pavilion. Square in shape and archaic in form, the pavilion is supported by stone columns and beams. Placed horizontally on the front beam of the pavilion is a tablet on which is inscribed the name of the pavilion — Cang Lang, meaning Surging Waves. This tablet is a relic of the Qian Long era of the Qing Dynasty. On the columns on the same side is inscribed a couplet which goes:

"The fresh breeze and the shining moon
are a free gift,
Nigh and afar the streams and hills
seem to have affections."

Standing on the eastern part of the miniature mountain, the pavilion is surrounded by verdant green. Looking around, one may wonder whether it is in a natural vale.

The miniature mountain lying in the middle of the garden compound can be divided into two parts. The eastern part is constructed mainly with *huangshi* granite, mixing rocks and earth. An apparition of a real mountain, its winding paths, streams and valleys create the scenery of a natural landscape. The western part is a natural landscape built out of *hushi* eroded limestone. At the foot is a huge rock inscribed with the words "liu yu", polished jade, which refer to the beauty of this miniature mountain.

To the south are two clusters of buildings. Of the east cluster, the Hall for Elucidating the Way (Ming Dao Tang) and World of the Immortals (Yao Hua Jing Jie) are the largest structures. The west cluster is composed of Fragrant Hall, Memorial Hall of Five Hundred Men of Virtues, Hall of the Utmost Respect (Yang Zhi Tang), Exquisite Green Hall and Lotus Pavilion. Together with many verandahs, they form a compound of various scenes.

At the southern tip of the garden is another miniature mountain, much smaller in size. On the top of the mountain, Mountain View Hall offers a good distant view of the scene to the north. Below the hall are two stone houses, in front of which is a rockery which bears the inscription "Yuan Ling zheng jian" (May the Garden God be my witness) in the handwriting of Lin Zexu, the official who destroyed the illegal opium of the British in 1839.

96

96. The classical Surging Wave Pavilion high on the top of a hill. Inscribed on the front columns is a couplet which goes, "The fresh breeze and the shining moon are a free gift,/ Nigh and afar the streams and hills seem to have affections."

98

97. A view of the Exquisite Green Hall with a bamboo grove right in front

98. Furniture inside the Ming Dao Hall. Archaic in form, they are carved out of tree roots.

99

99. Pavilion for the Royal Tablet. Displayed in the pavilion is a tablet inscribed with the calligraphy of the Qing emperor Kang Xi. (photograph by Chung Wah Nan)

100

101

102

100. A highly decorative brick lattice window
101. Lattice windows in the Garden of the Surging Wave Pavilion
102. Stone bridge over the pond before the garden

滄浪亭

Pleasure Garden

Originally part of the residence of Wu Kuan, Secretary of State of the Ming Dynasty, Pleasure Garden (Yi Yuan) was extended by Gu Zishan during the reign of the Qing emperor Guang Xu. Gu separated the garden into two parts with a double gallery. On the east side is the old garden of Wu Kuan while on the west side is the extension of Gu, the two parts totaling nine hectares.

As Pleasure Garden is the most recent of traditional Suzhou gardens, features of various older gardens were adopted in its construction. Its double gallery is modelled on that of Surging Wave Pavilion, the miniature mountain imitates that of Surrounding Beauty Villa (Huan Xiu Shan Zhuang) and its Lotus Pond takes Wang Shi Garden as exemplar. This garden provides an abundance of scenes within its limited space. To add to the garden's attraction, calligraphy by famous scholars and poets throughout history are displayed everywhere in an aura of elegance.

The west garden is the chief scenic region of the compound. In the center is a natural pond with meandering banks, and to its north is a miniature mountain on which the hexagonal Little Surging Wave Pavilion stands. Hanging on the columns of the pavilion are two wooden tablets inscribed with a couplet by the famous Ming poet-calligrapher Zhu Zhishan. The couplet goes:

''A world of bamboos brimming over with moonlight,
Pines sing together with the soothing wind.''

Behind the pavilion is a rare stone called the Three Layer Screen because of its shape.

To the south of the pond is a hall compound with its platform extending over the pond. The hall compound is made of two parts: the north is the Lotus Pavilion, an ideal spot for enjoying the lotus in summer; to the south is the Plum Blossom Hall (also known as Ploughing Moon Pavilion) where one can leisurely admire the spring plum blossoms and peonies. In the Lotus Pavilion the archaic furniture is made of box-wood and cedar *(Machilus nanmu).* To its west is a small building called Biwu Qifeng (Emerald Green Parasol Tree Where the Phoenix Perches). Inlaid above the lintel of a moon gate to its east are the characters ''dun ku'', meaning the place for the hermit, by the Qing calligrapher He Shaoji. On the walls of the front and left galleries of the former Moonlight Pavilion are inlaid stone tablets inscribed with the calligraphy of the famous poet-calligraphers Mi Fei of the Song Dynasty and Tang Yin of the Ming Dynasty.

To the west of the pond is Hua Fang Study (Study of the Gaily-Painted Plesure Boat). Heavy Dew Hall, also known as the Peony Hall, is positioned further west.

In the east garden, Jade Pavilion (Yu Yan Ting), Free and Easy Throughout the Seasons Pavilion (Sishi Xiaosa Ting), Lute House of Poxian, Stone Boat and Jade Rainbow Pavilion form courtyards of different sizes, connected to each other by galleries. Inside Jade Pavilion is a stone inscription of a couplet by the Ming artist Dong Qichang which goes:

''Sitting in solitude, I mediate on the mysterious,
In peace and quiet, I am glad to reside.''

Along the double gallery are lattice windows of rich patterns, and through the windows, the scenes on both sides can be observed.

103

103. A dainty court with the Sishi Xiaosa Pavilion in the background

怡園

105

104. The entrance. With plastered walls as a backdrop to the trees and rocks as well as the cave, the setting composes an attractive picture.

105. A gallery joining the double gallery in the background. A double gallery is one which is partitioned into two by a wall running along in the middle. On the wall are lattice windows which offer views from both sides.

106. A cave from the miniature mountain in front of Biwu Qifeng

Crane Garden

Crane Garden (He Yuan) is located at Han Jia Lane. Built in the late Qing Dynasty, it is about two *mu* (one *mu* equals 0.0667 hectares) in size.

The planning of Crane Garden is similar to that of *sihe yuan* living compounds in North China, which are enclosed by houses on four sides. Rooms are arranged along a north-south axis, thereby separating the garden into two major spaces.

Buildings on the two sides along the axis are of different forms and variant styles. Scattered here and there are ponds and bushes, producing a natural beauty.

The front hall is of five bays. After entering, one can see its plastered lattice windows rendered in exquisite designs. To its east is a zigzag gallery which sprawls to the north, linking the Square Hall and the north main hall. The Square Hall is in the middle toward south of the overall compound, dividing it into two parts.

The southern part is smaller in size and serves as a foil to the north section which is the scenic region of the compound. To the west of this scenic area is the double-eaved Trapezoid Hall with its peculiar shape. The hall portico joins the main hall in the north, and in the east the Square Pavilion rises in the middle part of zigzag gallery. One trapezoidal, one square, these buildings form an interesting combination. In the spaces between the east gallery and the wall surrounding the garden bamboos and flowers are planted. In the center is a naturally shaped pond, around which are rockeries of *hushi* eroded limestone. At the southwest of the pond, a bay forks out to join the hillock at the southwest. A small bridge spans over the bay. On the hillock is a little hexagonal pavilion which offers a panoramic view of the north garden. East of the main hall is a dainty courtyard. In the north is a studio which is connected to the zigzag gallery.

All over the garden flowers of all seasons blossom. Lilacs, Chinese flowering crabapples, osmanthus, roses, winter jasmins and magnolias all add hues and natural flavor to the garden.

107

107. A corner of the garden
108. A view of the garden with its structures lining up in a seemingly wriggling movement

Lotus-root Garden

Constructed in the early Qing Dynasty, it was originally known as the Ford Garden (She Yuan) which later fell into ruins. During the late Qing, the garden was reconstructed. As the east and west parts of the garden are shaped like a lotus-root, the garden was given its present name.

The east garden is rectangular with an area of four *mu.* In the north, the two-storied Chengqu Thatched Hut was the festive spot of the former owners. In front of the building is a lawn with a miniature mountain of *huangshi* granite which marks the chief scene of the garden.

The miniature mountain consists of two parts, divided by a valley. The east mountain is accessible by a stone path from the Thatched Hut. Planted all over with flowers and trees, the mountain is characterized by its ravines, cliffs and precipices which create such a feeling that "a foot of land appears to cover a whole mountain and a forest". Its rockeries rise and fall to form various rare and yet natural shapes, revealing the influence of Chinese painting. As such, the east mountain is regarded as a masterpiece of Suzhou miniature mountains. The west mountain is smaller, with gentler slopes. From between the two parts, the one-meter-wide valley cuts deeply down and is therefore called the "Deep Vale (Sui Gu)".

To the east of the miniature mountain is an elongated pond. At its southern tip, a spacious pavilion called Shan Shui Jian (Between the Hill and the Water) stands out over the water, facing the Thatched Hut in the far north. Inside the pavilion is an exquisitely carved screen with the characters "sui han san you" (the three winter friends, i.e. pine, bamboo and plum blossom, symbols of perseverance and loyalty to the Chinese). When one goes south along the bank, the precipitous valley on the west will come into sight before one passes onto the zigzag bridge twisting over the pond. To the east of the Shan Shui Jian, a stone path leads to the flower platform with a facing of *huangshi* granite. Bamboo groves, flowers and trees enliven the atmosphere. This elegant flower platform forms a strong contrast with the magnificent miniature mountain on the opposite side.

In the west garden, a study called the Zhilian Laowu (Old House for Screen Weaving) divides the garden into two parts. In the front part is a miniature mountain; at the back is a library. This is a good example of the style that combines a garden and a library in one compound.

109

110

111

109. Southern part of the elongated pond. Along the shore, a gallery zigzags through a small pavilion before it joins the Shan Shui Jian Pavilion at the back.

110. Scene outside Chengqu Thatched Hut (photograph by Feng Yunqing)

111. The miniature mountain. Piled up with ***huangshi*** *granite and covered densely with plants, it is as imposing as a natural rocky mountain.*

Yu Garden

Yu Garden is located in the Temple of the City God, Shanghai. During the Jia Jing and Wan Li eras of the Ming Dynasty, Pan Yunduan built this garden to please his father, hence the name "Yu Garden", "the garden to please". During the Ming Dynasty, much of the garden was destroyed and deserted. In the Qian Long period of the Qing, the garden was reconstructed and renamed West Garden. However, the greater part of it was later occupied by merchants and hawkers who made it a marketplace. It was not until 1958 that the garden was restored to its former beauty.

The area of Yu Garden is about 30 *mu* (one *mu* equals 0.0667 hectares), with walls separating the garden into courts of different sizes and characteristics. The observers' walkway twists and turns all through the garden, creating a feeling of much enlarged size.

Turning north after entering the front gate, one comes to the garden's scenic area which comprises the Three Grain Ear Hall (Sansui Hall), Lofty Mount Hall (Yangshan Hall), Rolling up the Rain Mansion (Zhuanyu Mansion), a lotus pond and a miniature mountain. The miniature mountain is built of *huangshi* granite and is the creation of the famous rock mountain master Zhang Nanyang of the Ming Dynasty. The mountain is grand and forceful; from the Lofty Mount Hall across the lotus pond in the south, a view typical of Chinese landscape paintings can be observed. On the tip of the mountain is a small pavilion named "Viewing the River (Wan Jiang)". From this vantage point one can see the Huangpu River from afar.

To the east of the lotus pond is the Gallery Leading Gradually into Beauty (Jianru Jiajing Gallery). Following the gallery to the north and turning east, there is a small and narrow court with an arched wall spanning the pond. Its image, together with the flowers and rocks and nearby structures, is mirrored in the water. This scene is so beautiful that it gives one a feeling of entering a painting.

Further east is a cluster of buildings arranged along a clear-cut axis. With the Ten Thousand Flower Mansion as the principle structure, the cluster comprises the Library (Cangshu Lou), Heralding Spring Hall, Opera Terrace (Da Chang Tai) and the Geniality Hall. The Heralding Spring Hall was used as the headquarters for a peasant rebellion organized by the Small Sword Society in 1855.

To the east of this cluster of built structures are a miniature mountain, a pond and several pavilions. Natural and simple, they enliven the whole atmosphere and balance the formal air of the main buildings.

Going on and passing the west wall through the vase-shaped gate, one enters the Hui Jing area. The vista is grand and open here, with the Nine Lion Pavilion, Hexagonal Pavilion, Hui Jing Mansion, Possessing the Moon Mansion (De Yue Mansion) and Resplendent Jade Hall centering around a lotus pond. In front of the Resplendent Jade Hall is a peak of rather large size but nevertheless delicate and punched with holes. Known as the Delicate Jade, it is believed to be a tribute to Emperor Hui Zong of the Song Dynasty.

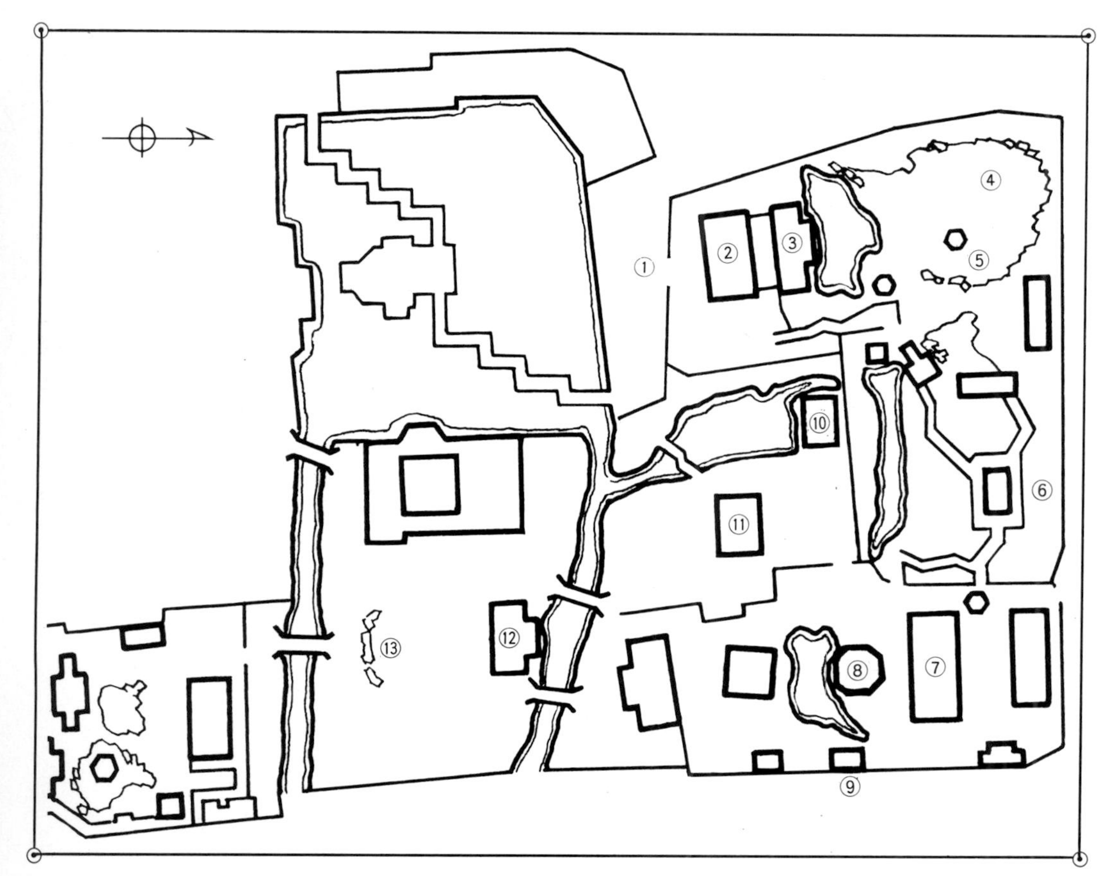

Yu Garden
1. *entrance*
2. *Three Grain Ear Hall*
3. *Rolling Up the Rain Pavilion*
4. *miniature mountain*
5. *Pavilion for Viewing the River*
6. *Thousand Flower Pavilion*
7. *Heralding Spring Hall*
8. *Opera Terrace*
9. *Kuai Mansion*
10. *Nine Lion Pavilion*
11. *Possessing the Moon Mansion*
12. *Resplendent Jade Hall*
13. *Delicate Jade Rockery*

112

113

114

112. The miniature mountain with Wanjiang Pavilion on its top. Grand and imposing, it embodies the artistic conception of Chinese landscape painting. A stone path leads up to its top.

113. Nine Lion Pavilion. Built of stone, its balcony stretches out into the water.

114. Dragon Wall. At the end of the wall a dragon's head proudly raises high. The tiles covering the wall top suggest the scales of its body. Rising up and down as the traditional wave-shaped cloud wall, it is also known as Dragon in Cloud Wall. (photograph by Yau Kam)

115

115. Chinese garden-makers make good use of cave-gates to connect different scenes. With variant shapes, cave-gates form attractive scene frames. Shown here is one with a vase shape.
116. Kuai Hall on the miniature mountain east of Heralding Spring Hall

Qing Hui Garden

Situated in Daliang City, Shunde County, Qing Hui Garden (Clear Sunlight Garden) is the largest in scale among the gardens in the Yangtze region. It was built in the Qian Long period of the Qing Dynasty and subsequently extended to its present size.

Inside the garden are arranged the Guiji Hut (Return Home Hut), Xiyin Study (Value the Time Study), Bishenghua Hall (Master Stroke Hall), Chun Ting (Floating Hall) and other buildings in an original pattern. The Floating Hall was modeled on the floating mansions in the Pearl River region. Looking down from the hall at the lake surface in the front, one seems to be floating on the sea.

The three ponds in the garden are of different shapes. On one side of the rectangular pond, the small Clear Wave Pavilion stands out above the water while the Hexagonal Pavilion also extends into the pond, breaking up the straight shoreline and producing a hint of irregularity. The Clear Wave Pavilion is a vantage point for watching fish. On the other side of the pond, a loquat tree with its golden fruit makes a fascinating reflection. Throughout the garden are plants commonly found in South China, such as the lily, magnolia, jasmine, longan, litchi and banana.

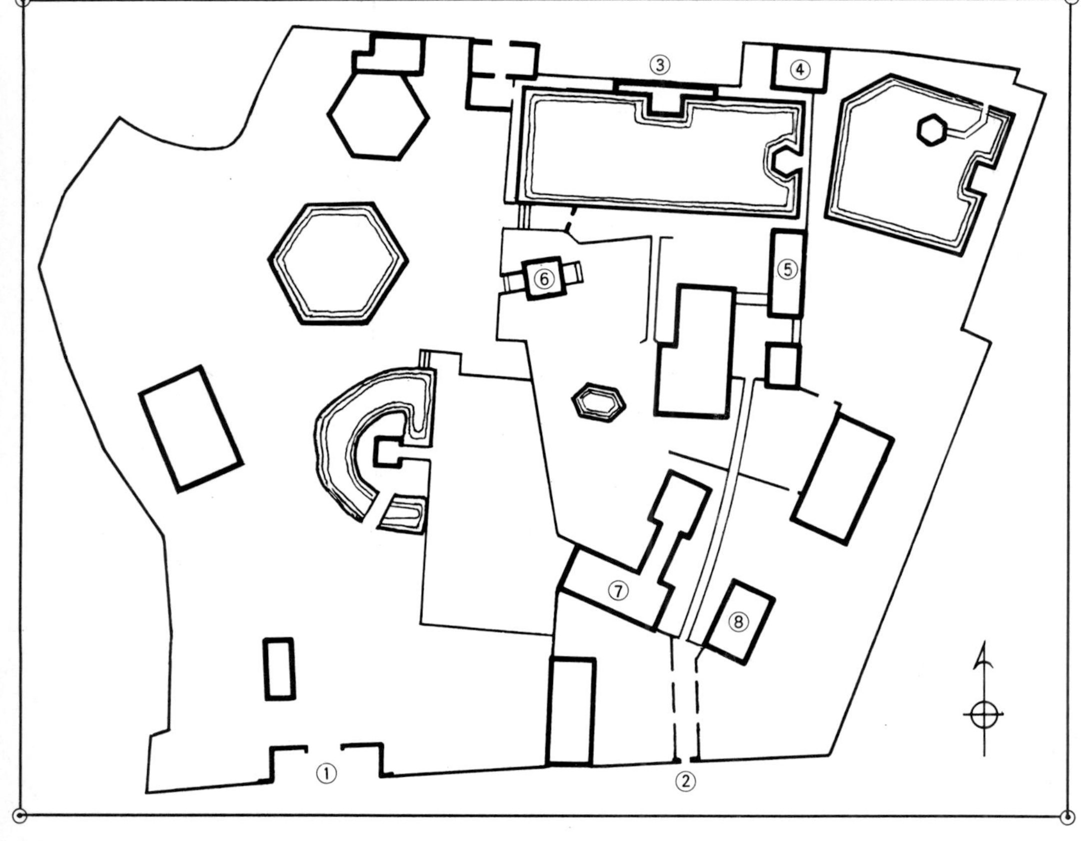

Qing Hui Garden
1. *entrance*
2. *back gate*
3. *Clear Wave Pavilion*
4. *Thatched Hut of Clear Lake*
5. *Chu Xiang Garden*
6. *pavilion*
7. *Return Home Hut*
8. *Master Stroke Hall*

117

117. The Floating Hall and its flight of steps piled up with rocks

118. The Clear Wave Pavilion and Hexagonal Pavilion breaking the straight shoreline of the rectangular pond, producing a hint of irregularity.

119

120

119. A moon gate at the end of the entrance path flanked by trees

120. The court in the south of the Floating Hall. Its colorful window frames and balustrades exquisitely carved, the building is typical of the Lingnan garden.

Ke Garden (Dongguan)

Built in the Qing Dynasty, the garden is located at Boxia Village in the west suburb of Dongguan County, Guangdong Province. It was originally the villa of the Qing official Zhang Jingxiu.

Though the garden is only three *mu* in area, the structures inside are numerous and the views full of changes. Scattered among the pavilions, terraces, ponds, bridges, and halls are rockeries and flowers.

Passing through the entrance gate, one enters Peeling-Red-Peel Pavilion (Bo Hong Pavilion). Joining the pavilion is a zigzag bridge, along which the views of the garden gradually unroll before the visitor. Moon Worshipping Pavilion, Cave of the Immortals, Orchid Pavilion and a meandering pond all do their best to attract attention.

In the garden there was originally a rockery standing by the pond in the shape of a carpenter's square. The rockery was known as the ''Unicorn Playing with the Moon'', probably for its peculiar shape. Spanning over the pond now is an arch bridge. Leaning on its balustrades, one can leisurely watch the lotus and fish below. By the side of the pond is a little court with a ''half-pavilion'' built on its side known as Bo Hong Pavilion, or Peeling-Red-Peel Pavilion, as it is the place where people used to feast on the litchi planted in the court.

The most important structure is a four-storied building. The ground floor encompasses Laurel hall and the Shuang Qing Hall. And as the plan looks like the character *ya* (亞), the ground floor is also called the Ya Shape Hall. The top floor is Yan Shan House (House for Playing Host to Mounts), from which a panoramic view of the landscape in the Boxia Village can be obtained.

At the back of the garden is a natural pond. Standing by the pond, silhouetted against the distant hills and fields are a pavilion, zigzag bridges and floating halls. The skill of ''view borrowing'' is successfully applied.

121

122

123

124

121. Side view of the Ya Shape Hall. Standing by a lotus pond, it is accessible by a little arch bridge.
122. A view through the moon gate
123. Shuangqing Hall viewed from the lotus pond to its north
124. The court where Peeling-Red-Peel Pavilion can be found

Yu Yin Villa

Situated in Nan Cun, Panyu County, Guangdong Province and built in the Tong Zhi period of the Qing, the villa is divided into two parts by a bridge in the middle. The eastern part comprises a rectangular water court, inside which a rectangular pond is surrounded by rockeries. On the south of the pond is an ancillary hall with its porch stretching out over the water. On the north is the Dense Willow Hall (Shen Liu Tang) which is the main hall of the whole compound. The decorations and interior design are typical of the Lingnan region. Inscribed on the sandalwood on its north side are calligraphy and paintings of famous scholars. The lattice screens on the east and west sides are carved with designs of litchi, a common theme in the Lingnan region. Inlaid on the window on the south side are colorful glazed panes with floral designs. When seen through the window, the floating clouds, flowers and trees seem peculiarly beautiful. Outside the hall is an iron frame in floral design.

In the center of the west court is the Dainty Water Pavilion. The pavilion is connected with other structures by a gallery which spans all the way over a hexagonal pond. Around the pond are rockeries and plants. The ponds on both sides are linked by a gallery bridge. Partitioning the garden into two parts, the bridge adds to the depth of field of the surrounding scenes. Running in the midst of a world of flowers and greenery with a stream flowing below, the bridge is called "Washing the Red (Huanhong) and Spanning into Greenery (Kualü)".

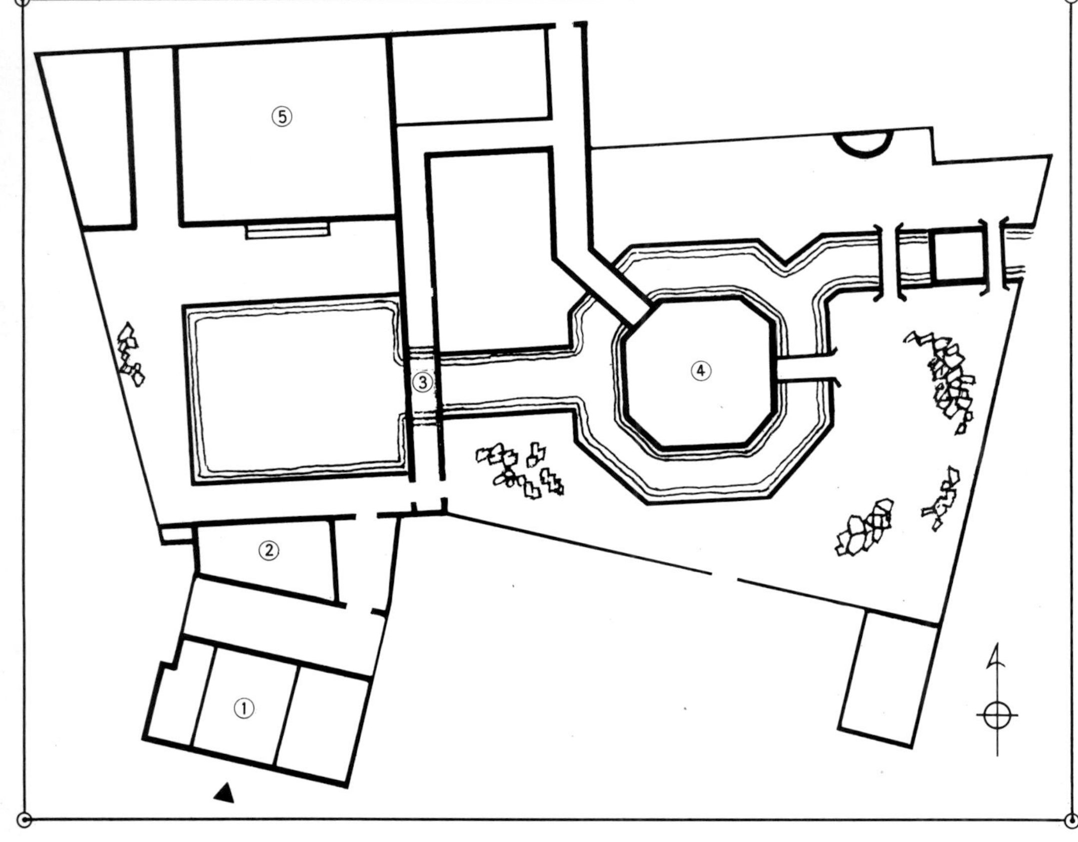

Yu Yin Villa
1. *front hall*
2. *waterside hall*
3. *Washing-the-Red Bridge*
4. *Dainty Water Pavilion*
5. *Dense Willow Hall*

125

125. Washing-the-Red Bridge

126

127

128

126. Iron frame with floral designs outside the main hall
127. Glazed window in the main hall
128. Octagonal Pavilion

Natural Scenic Parks and Temple Gardens

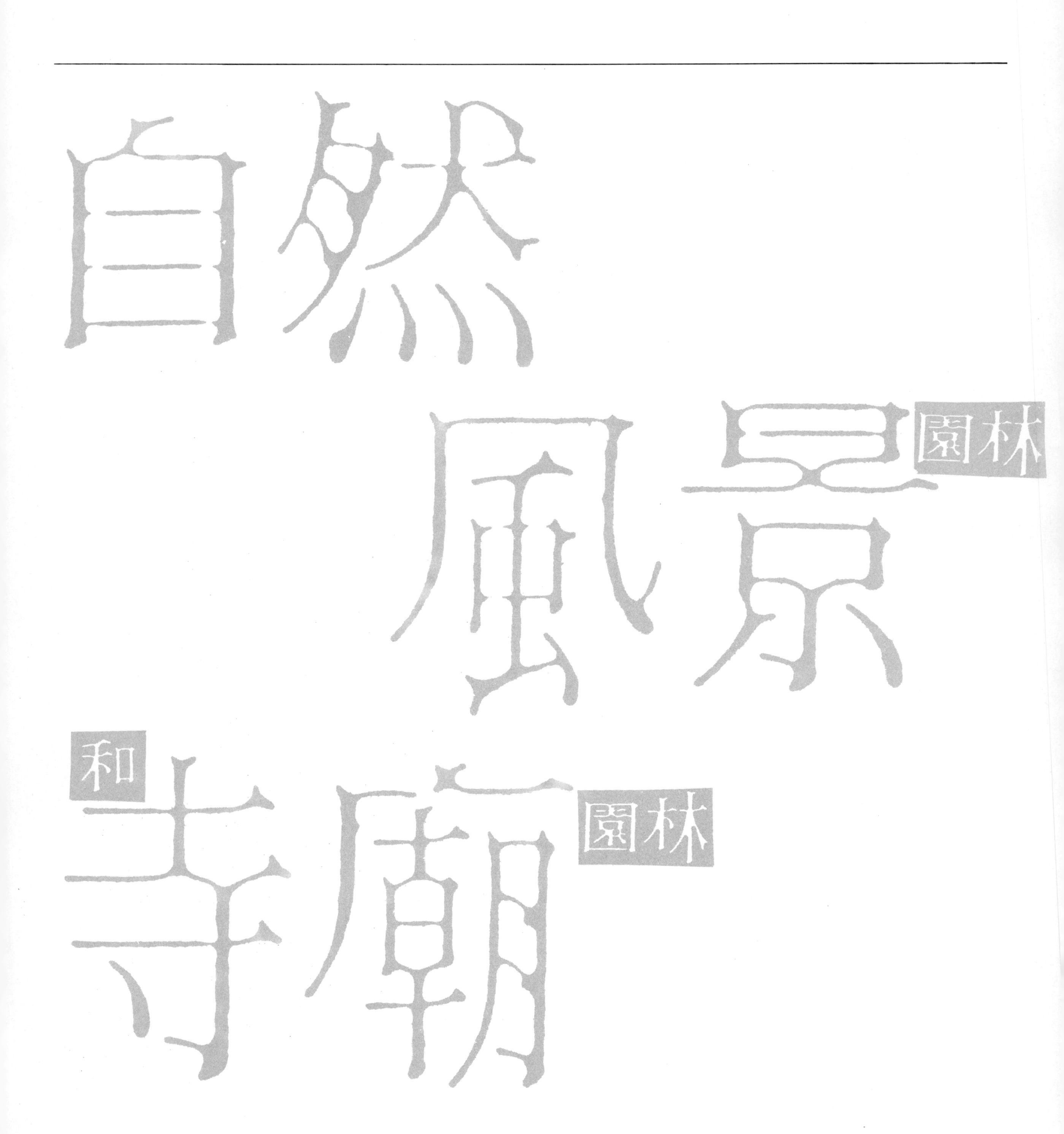

Tan Zhe Temple

Tan Zhe Temple (Temple of the Pond and Cudrania) is one of the most famous Buddhist temples in Beijing. It is situated in the western suburb on the side of Tan Zhe Mountain. On the mountain are the Dragon Pond *(long tan)* and many cudrania trees *(zhe)* which account for the name of the mountain and the temple.

Tan Zhe Temple has a long history. A Beijing adage has it that ''at first there was the Tan Zhe before there was the city''. The temple has many names. During the Jin Dynasty (265-420), it was known as the Jia Fu Temple; during the Tang Dynasty it was called the Dragon Spring Temple; during the Jin Dynasty (1115-1234) it was renamed as the Great Longevity Temple, and in Ming times it was given the ancient name of Jia Fu again; in Qing times, this was changed to Flowing Clouds Temple. The common people, however, have always called it Tan Zhe Temple, and this is the name that comes down to us today. The extant structures are mainly left from the Ming and Qing periods.

The temple was built following the contour of the mountain. Along a north-south axis are three main groupings of courts and halls. In the middle cluster, starting from the entrance arch, is the Lokapala Hall (Tian Wang Dian), the main hall, the Three Buddha Hall, the Hall of Fasting and the Vairocana Pavilion (Pilu Pavilion). Following the elevation of the mountain, the buildings stagger upwards. Within the garden, there are tall ancient trees which seem to be touching the sky, while green grass blankets the ground. In the front of the Three Buddha Hall is a grand tall ginkgo tree which is also known as the Emperor Tree. Legend has it that it was planted during the Liao Dynasty (916-1125) and has a history of nearly one thousand years. Still growing strong, it provides leafy shade for the courtyard. Vairocana Pavilion is a building of two stories, standing on the highest point of the whole compound. From this pavilion the view of the surrounding landscape and the whole temple is spectacular.

On the left side are the Priests' Court and the Qing emperor's travel lodge which comprises such buildings as the Long-lived-emperor's Hall, the Empress Dowager's Hall, the Pavilion of Floating Glass, the Bamboo Pond, etc. The size of the structures is comparatively small, and the courtyard gardens are quiet and peaceful. Bamboo groves spread over the area, and the natural streams are deep and clear. The Pavilion of Floating Glass was built to carry on the tradition of ''float the wine vessel in a meandering brook and drink the wine when the vessel stops'', prevalent during the Han and Wei dynasties. On the right side is a cluster of temples and halls such as the Leng Yan Altar, Jie Altar and Guan Yin Hall. At the back of the temple is the Dragon Pond with a diameter of about three meters. The water is crystalline with the bottom visible, and the flow of the spring never stops.

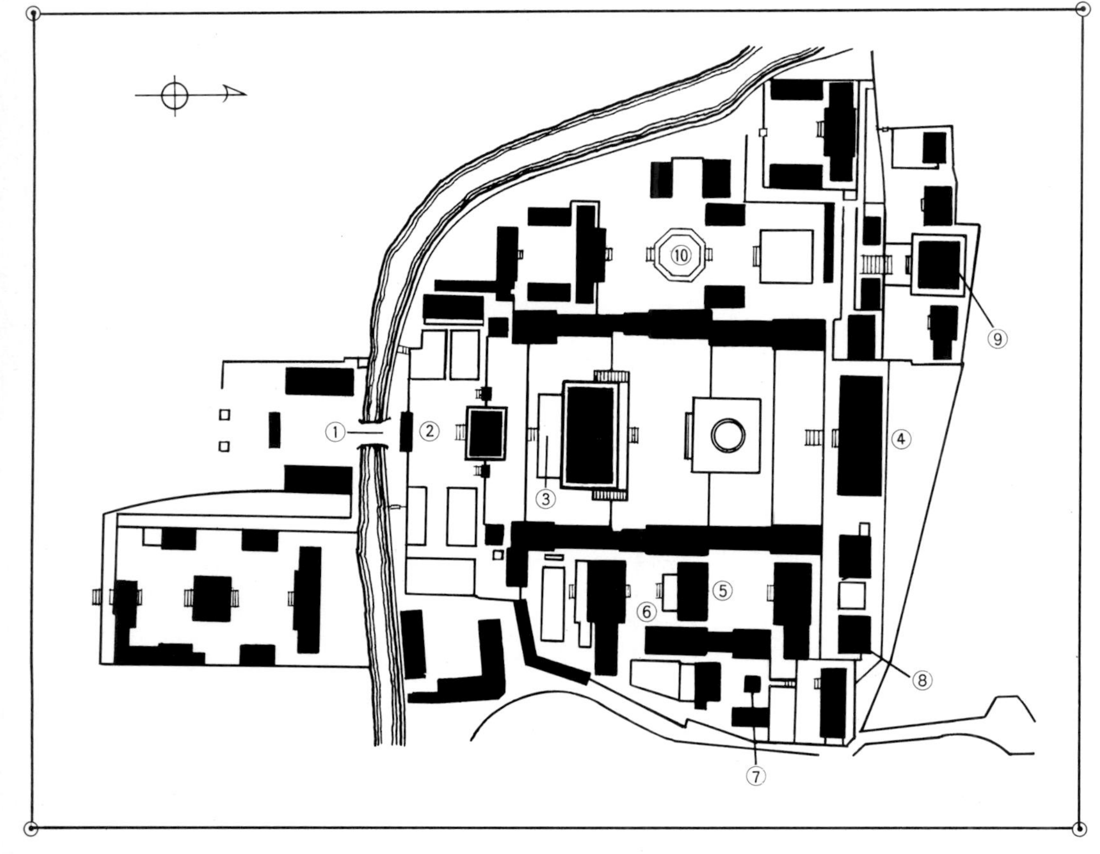

Tan Zhe Temple
1. *entrance*
2. *Lokapala Hall*
3. *main hall*
4. *Vairocana Pavilion*
5. *Hall of the God of Fortunes*
6. *Empress Dowager's Hall*
7. *Pavilion of Floating Glass*
8. *Emperor Qian Long's Seat*
9. *Guan Yin Hall*
10. *Leng Yan Altar*

129

129. The main gate. A beamless hall of brick wall construction, it makes a beautiful scene together with the Tan Zhe Mountain at its back.

130. The main hall. In front of the hall is a terrace with white marble balustrades. On the main ridge-pole, the end ornaments in the shape of a bird's tail rise 2.9 meters. The hardy, old pines standing in the front add to its magnificence.

131

131. Exterior view of the Pilu Pavilion. The last building along the middle grouping, it is the temple for the Buddha Pilushene, or Vairocana in Sanskrit.

132. The gingko tree, given the name ''Emperor Tree'' by Emperor Qian Long of the Qing, is said to have been planted first during the Liao Dynasty. It is more than 30 meters in height and four meters in diameter.

Great Awakening Temple

Great Awakening Temple is situated on the western edge of Yang Tai Mountain (Sunny Platform) which is linked to Western Mountain. The views are extremely beautiful. During the Liao Dynasty, Clear Water Court was built. In the Jin Dynasty (1115-1234), it became one of the eight great gardens of Western Mountain. During early Ming Dynasty, it was expanded, and was again expanded and refurbished during the reigns of the Qing emperors Yong Zheng and Qian Long. What is preserved today is from the Qing times.

Great Awakening Temple consists of two clusters of buildings plus a garden forest area. The structures are arranged on parallel east-west axes, all facing east, stemming from the habits of the Liao people who like to orient themselves towards the sun. Along the main axis there is the Maitreya Hall, the main hall and the Dong Jing Deng Guan Temple, all grand and tall Buddhist temples. Inside the garden of Dong Jing Deng Guan Temple is a thousand-year-old ginkgo tree standing straight and proud with luxuriant branches and rustling leaves. On the other axis were built the recreational places of the imperial family. The main structures are Si Yi Hall and the Rest Pavilion for Clouds. In front of the Rest Pavilion are cleverly designed stone steps and rockeries of high artistic value.

Along the hillside at the back of these two clusters of buildings is a beautiful garden. In the south of the garden, the Pavilion of Leading Importance stands prominently on a high spot. On the northern highland is a white Lamaist pagoda. Built during the time of the Emperor Qian Long, the pagoda established the main image for the Great Awakening Temple. Behind the pagoda is a lotus pond and pavilions. Along the two sides of the hill are stone steps with brooks flowing alongside. With trees and vines shading the sun, green grass thriving and wild flowers blooming in the breeze, the garden radiates natural beauty.

133

133. *Dong Jing Deng Guan Temple, main structure of the compound*

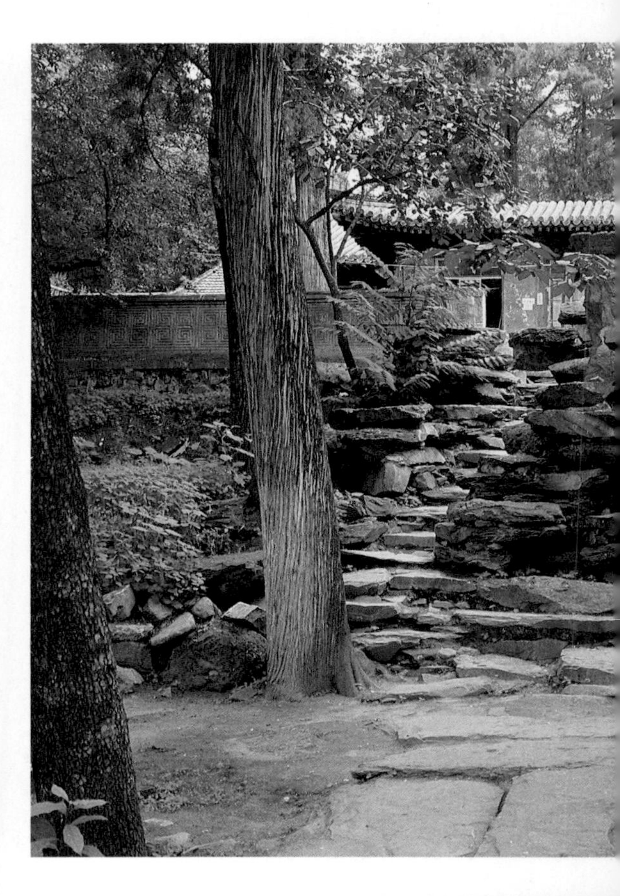

134

135

136

137

134. Artificial rockeries integrated harmoniously with steps of natural stone
135. Stone steps in the compound of the Great Enlightenment Temple
136. The slope at the back of the compound
137. Stone path at the back of the garden. Running in the midst of trees and bamboo, it is full of rustic flavor.

Great Brightness Lake

Great Brightness Lake was first mentioned in the authoritative *Shui Jing Zhu (Notes on ''The Book of Waters'')* by the Northern Wei geographer Li Daoyuan. Its water surface vast, the lake was known as Lotus Seed Lake during the Six Dynasties. In Sui and Tang times, it was known as Li Shui Lake. During the fifth year of the reign of the Song emperor Shen Zong, the celebrated writer Zeng Gong took over the governance of Jinan. To utilize the water, he built many dams around the lake, thereby shrinking its size. What was left then has become the Great Brightness Lake of today. Situated in the immediate north of the center of Jinan city, the lake covers an area of 46 hectares, the water coming from 72 famous springs and streams.

With its water shining in great beauty and the surrounding landscape swelling with charm, Great Brightness Lake has ''knocked over'' generations of poets and painters with its scenery. Lots of poems and calligraphy were written in praise of this alluring lake. A vivid and detailed description can be found in Liu E's *Travel Notes of Old Cán.* The temples, ancestral halls and garden architecture in its surroundings add to its beauty and make it one of the most famous natural scenic gardens in China.

There are many historical relics and famous buildings around the lake. To the south are Reverie Garden, the Memorial Temple of the Southern Song poet Xin Jiaxuan and the provincial library. On the northern bank are the Memorial Temple of the Ming official Tie Xuan, the Northermost Pavilion, South Sumptuous Temple and Wave Confluence Bridge. In the middle of the lake are Li Xia Pavilion, Spring Confluence Hall and Lake Center Pavilion as well as six small islands.

Reverie Garden was built during the first year of the Qing emperor Xuan Tong after the style of Glimpse of the Sky Pavilion in Lingbo, known for its miniature mountains, pavilions and bridges. The meandering walkways are particularly quiet and mysterious. The ancient trees grow so close they seem to be embracing one another. On a miniature hill by the lake stands Noble Spirit Garden which is the scenic spot on the south bank of the lake.

Li Xia Pavilion is located on the largest island. Around the island are planted weeping willows. With its red columns and flying roof standing elegantly among the greenery, the pavilion is the shining pearl of the lake. Built in the Northern Wei Dynasty, it was repaired substantially during the early Qing. At the entrance of the pavilion hangs a couplet which goes:

''Archaic is this pavilion at the west of the lake.

How full of brilliant scholars is Jinan''

Written in the handwriting of the Qing calligrapher He Shaoji, this couplet is taken from the poem that the great Tang poet Du Fu wrote to his friend Li Yong.

South Sumptuous Temple is situated at the northeastern shore of the lake. It was built to commemorate the famous writer Zeng Gong who had ruled Jinan for some time. Standing by the lake, it is a hall open on four sides. At the back side is a lotus pond, and behind the pond is a verdant bamboo grove.

Built during the Qian Long period of the Qing Dynasty in commemoration of Tie Xuan, the minister of war of the Ming Dynasty who died when fighting against a usurper, the Memorial Temple of Tie Xuan is situated on the northwest shore. With pavilions, porches and bridges, it forms an independent garden. Near the lake is the Little Surging Wave Pavilion and a long corridor. Behind the pavilion is a lotus pond. From the pavilion one can have the best picture of the Thousand Buddha Mountain's reflection in the water. Along the walls of the corridor stone carvings of calligraphy are embedded. The best known one goes:

''In the midst of the green green willows
colorful lotuses bloom all around;
Among a city of verdant mountains
the lake sings in a soft light sound.''

Written in the handwriting of Tie Bao, the couplet is enjoyed and repeated by visitors.

The Northernmost Pavilion, also known as the Northernmost Temple, is located at the east of the northern shore. A Taoist temple, it is a group of buildings constructed on a high platform. It was built in the Yuan Dynasty and repaired during the Ming Dynasty. In front of the pavilion is a high platform from which one can have a view of the whole lake.

138

138. The Great Brightness Lake

139

140

139. Li Xia Pavilion on the largest island in the lake. It became famous for the couplet by Du Fu, the greatest Tang poet. The couplet goes: "Archaic is this pavilion at the west of the lake,/How full of brilliant scholars is Jinan."

140. The long gallery joining Little Surging Wave Pavilion and Memorial Temple of Tie Xuan

141

141. Entrance and corridor of Reverie Garden
142. Full Green Pond surrounded by rocks. In the distance is the Hao Ran Pavilion

142

Jumping Splashing Spring

Jinan is known as the City of Springs, as it has 72 beautiful springs, and the Jumping Splashing Spring comes first among them. It is situated at the center of the city, and has a very long history. It was first recorded during the Northern Wei Dynasty in Li Daoyuan's *Notes on "The Book of Waters"*.

After 1949, Jumping Spashing Spring was enlarged and made into a garden. Waters from various springs such as the Jade Washing, Running Horse, Golden Thread, Willow Catkin, and Washing Bowl, are linked to the Jumping Splashing to make a beautiful water network and they make the garden a fascinating one.

A famous tourist spot, Jumping Splashing Spring now comprises many structures. The water of the spring flows into a pond around which are stone banisters. To the north stands the Li Yuan Hall (originally the Immortal Lü Zu's Temple) and Memorial Hall of the Goddess Eying, both popular temples and famous tourist spots. Li Yuan Hall was built in the Song Dynasty. *Li* is the name of a river, and *yuan* means source. It has been renovated many times. The present hall was built in the Qing Dynasty. Hanging on the pillars of an affiliated building in front of the hall is a couplet composed by the Yuan poet Zhao Mengfu:

> "Misty foggy the scene floats amidst a world of clouds,
> Roaring like a thunder the spring shakes the Great Brightness (to its north)"

It vividly describes the late autumn scene at Jumping Splashing. On a cold autumn day when the wind is calm, the surface of the spring is enveloped in a mist, probably because the water is warmer than the air, and the Li Yuan Hall appears to be floating in the clouds.

To the southwest is the Billow Watching Pavilion. In the front of the pavilion is a stone tablet, engraved on which are the words "Bao Tu Quan (Jumping Splashing Spring)". At the back, another tablet with the words "Guan Lan (Billow Watching)" inscribed on it marks the pavilion. Leaning on the banisters of the pavilion, one can leisurely enjoy the scene of the spring.

To the east of the spring is the Bridge for Crane Watching, in front of which is a stone arch inscribed with the words "Lian Shan Jiu Ji (ancient Site of Lotus Mount)". Going south from the bridge, one comes to a porch covered by flowers and leaves. Turning left and passing over a small arch bridge, Surging Wave Garden comes into sight. The garden was the studying place of the Ming poet Li Panlong.

To the west of the Jumping Splashing Spring is another beautiful spring, the Jade Washing. Its water splashing down through the cracks of the rockeries with a delightful sound, Jade Washing Spring deserves such a beautiful name. Lying to its north is the site which is believed to be where the Song poetess Li Qingzhao lived. This site is now turned into the Li Qingzhao Memorial Hall.

143

143. Maple River and Maple Pavilion

144

144. Golden Thread Spring
145. The long renowned Jumping Splashing Spring

145

Thousand Buddha Hill

Thousand Buddha Temple is located at the mid-level of Thousand Buddha Hill to the southwest of Jinan. Originally known as the Temple of the Thousand Buddha Hill, it was first built in the Sui Dynasty. During the Tang Dynasty it was reconstructed and renamed the Zen Temple of Fostering the Nation. It is composed of two parts. The west portion is known as Thousand Buddha Temple, the name the whole structure shares; the east area is the Li Shan Garden.

Thousand Buddha Temple has its entrance in the west. At the entrance is an arch with a signboard "Cloud Path and Zen Pass". After entering, one encounters a steep rocky cliff to the south, on which are ten grottos. With over one hundred statues of buddhas, this is the famous Thousand Buddha Cliff. Most of the statues are works of the Sui Dynasty. Finely sculptured, they are all beautiful in form. Among the grottos, Spring of Dragon, Pure Land and Qián Lou are the most famous. The temples and courts were built mostly near the northern cliff. Those which have been preserved to this day are Stone Tablets Porch, Tang Huai Pavilion, Stone Arch and Dui Hua Pavilion.

In the eastern part, Li Shan Garden has its own entrance. The major structures all face north, with the mountain in the background. They include Pavilion of the God of Literature (Wen Chang Pavilion), Lu Ban Memorial Hall and Emperor Shun Memorial Hall. There is also a cypress tree from the Song Dynasty. To the north alongside the cliff are a newly built long porch and the Good View Pavilion which is the best place to enjoy the scenery of the City of Springs.

In the old days, during the lunar calendar of Double Third, Double Seventh (when the cowherd and weaver maid meet in heaven) and Double Ninth, the city folk all climb the hill for enjoyment.

146

146. Thousand Buddha Grotto in the compound of Xing Guo Temple, Thousand Buddha Hill

147

148

147. Courtyard of the Thousand Buddha Temple
148. Gateway leading to the temple
149. Song Cypress in Li Shan Garden

Mochou Lake

Mochou Lake is situated outside Shui Xi Gate. The lake surface is about 30 hectares. In legend, it was named after a Southern Qi lady, Lu Mochou. In *Record of the Peaceful World (Taiping Huanyu Ji)* Mochou Lake was already mentioned. The shore of the lake is lined with misty willows, the vista touching and soft. Famous already in the Song and Yuan dynasties, Mochou Lake is known as the First Scenic Spot of Jinling Prefecture and the First Lake of Nanjing.

On the southern shore, there are three groups of courtyard houses which are connected with one another. The west cluster comprises the Lotus Appreciation Hall, Square Pavilion, and Bright Glory Pavilion. In the middle is a fish pond, at the center of which stands the statue of the girl after whom the lake is named. On the north wall of the Lotus Appreciation Hall is a huge window. Framing the Lake Center Pavilion within its brackets and connecting the visual space inside and outside of the court, the window helps to create a bright and crisp ambience. In the central cluster is the small court of Tulip Hall (Yu Jin Tang), supposedly the living chamber of Mochou. The east cluster consists of the Winning Chess Hall and Hua Yan Nunnery. Spread about here and there are rockeries, plants and flowers, creating a casual but elegant atmosphere. It is said that the first emperor of the Ming Dynasty Zhu Yuanzhang once played chess with his general Xu Da in the Winning Chess Hall. Today the hall serves as an exhibition space for furniture, bronze wares, paintings and calligraphy of the Ming and Qing Dynasties.

After the establishment of the People's Republic, more lakeside pavilions and lofts were constructed and trees planted everywhere. The Mochou Lake has become the major park of the city of Nanjing.

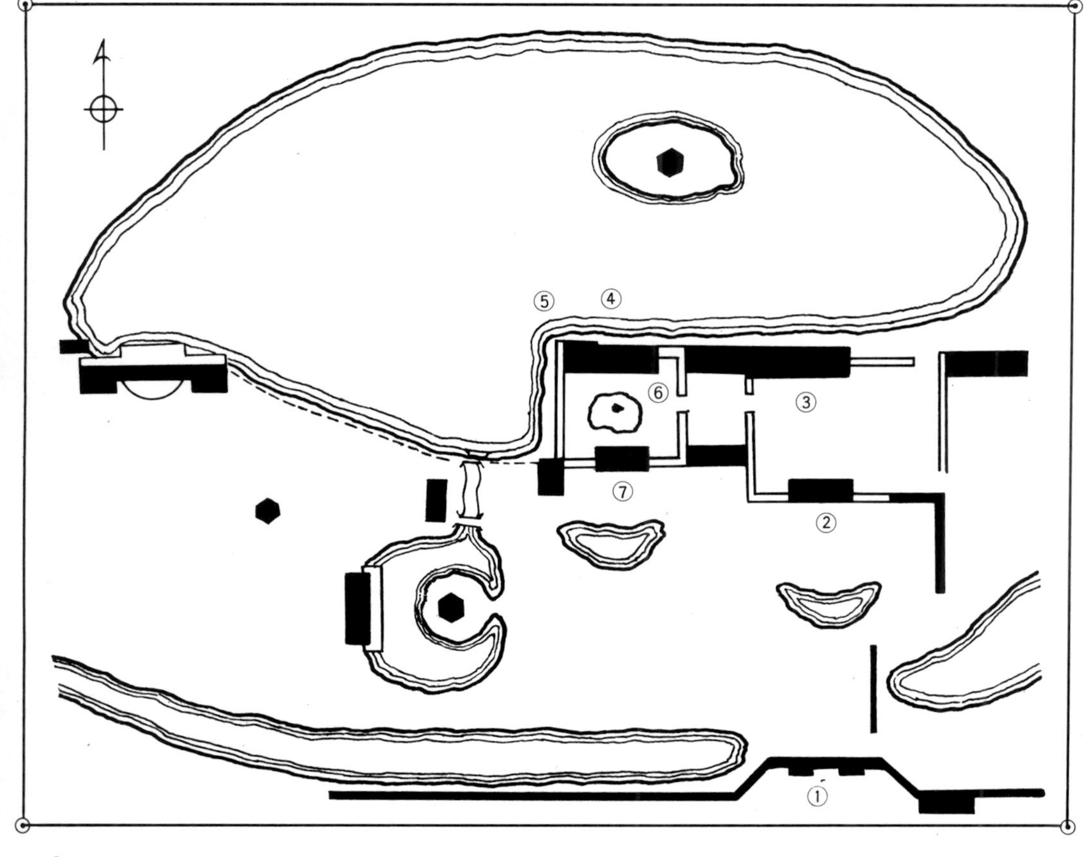

Mochou Lake
1. *entrance*
2. *Hua Yan Nunnery*
3. *Winning Chess Pavilion*
4. *Lotus Appreciation Hall*
5. *Square Pavilion*
6. *statue of Mochou*
7. *Bright Glory Pavilion*

150

150. Statue of Lady Mochou standing elegantly by the fish pond in front of Lotus Appreciation Hall

151

152

153

151. The west co[illegible]t of Winning Chess Hall
152. Winning Ch[illegible]s Hall, the place where the first Ming e[illegible]peror Zhu Yuanzhang once played chess [illegible]ith his general Xu Da.
153. Square Pavili[illegible] and Lotus Appreciation Hall viewed [illegible]m the lake's south bank

Slender West Lake

The Slender West Lake is located in the northwest of Yangzhou city. Originally known as the Protective River, it was formed from old city moats and ancient waterways. Since Sui and Tang times, it has gradually developed into a scenic area. When the Qing emperor Qian Long in his many trips to the south visited Slender West Lake, man-made scenic spots suddenly prospered around it. At the time, buildings and halls lined the lake shore, with pavilions and lofts in profusion. Along the shore, there are said to have been 24 scenic spots. A poem vividly describes the scene:

> ''Along the shores flowers and willows gently caress the water;
> Along the paths pavilions and terraces stretch towards the Mount.''

The Mount here refers to the Level Mount Hall on the west shore of the lake.

The entrance to this scenic park is the Great Rainbow Bridge, which was originally one of the 24 Scenes. The old saying goes:

> ''Yangzhou is good,
> And first comes Rainbow Bridge.''

After crossing the bridge and turning north one comes to a long causeway. Along the causeway weeping willows dance in the breeze, composing the famous scene of ''the long long causeway in the midst of weeping willows in spring.'' Green and fresh, the willows make an impressionistic painting of water and ink.

At the northern end of the causeway is the small Xu Garden. The main hall of the garden is named Listening to Oriole Hall. To the west stands the Poetic Spring Scene Pavilion, and further west, a corridor leads to the Carved Peak Chamber. In the front of the chamber, man-made peaks and rare rockeries form a refreshing vision of tranquillity.

From Xu Garden, a small bridge leads north to Little Golden Mount Island. Surrounded by water, the Little Golden Mount is situated at the center of the whole scenic park. It is created from earth excavated during the making of canals and was originally called the Everlasting Spring Mount. On the island is a hillock with a pavilion on its top. From the pavilion, which is called the Wind, the whole vista of the lake is in view.

On the western part of the island the Green Shade Chamber and Thatched Hut on the Lake make a fascinating sight. From the Thatched Hut a view to the west can be obtained. In the middle, there is Lute Chamber and Little Osmanthus Garden. In the east is Moon Pavilion with a beautiful distant view of Year-round Misty Rainy Mansion. A long causeway on the west of the island extends towards the center of the lake, at the end of which is Breezy Terrace. It is said that the Qing emperor Qian Long once fished here. The three sides of Breezy Terrace are yellow walls with moon gates. Their form and colors are in harmony with Five Pavilion Bridge in the west of the lake.

Five Pavilion Bridge, also called the Lotus Bridge, constitutes the main scene on the water. Built at the time of emperor Qian Long, its construction is complicated, with 15 arches. On the bridge are five pointed-roof pavilions with glazed yellow tiles. Their form is unusual and exceptionally fine, and this is the only one of its kind in traditional Chinese gardens.

To the south of Five Pavilion Bridge stands Lotus Spirit Temple. In this temple compound, there is a white Lamaist dagoba similar in shape to the White Dagoba in Beijing's Bei Hai Park, though more dainty and more slender. Together with Five Pavilion Bridge, the Lotus Spirit Temple produces a complex and intriguing profile, forming the hallmark image of the Slender West Lake.

To the east of Five Pavilion Bridge is a small island known as Wild Duck House, on which are lakeside pavilions and meandering corridors in an extremely pleasant environment. To the north, there is another building known as Water Cloud Magnanimity Hall or Big Osmanthus Hall which adds to the scenery.

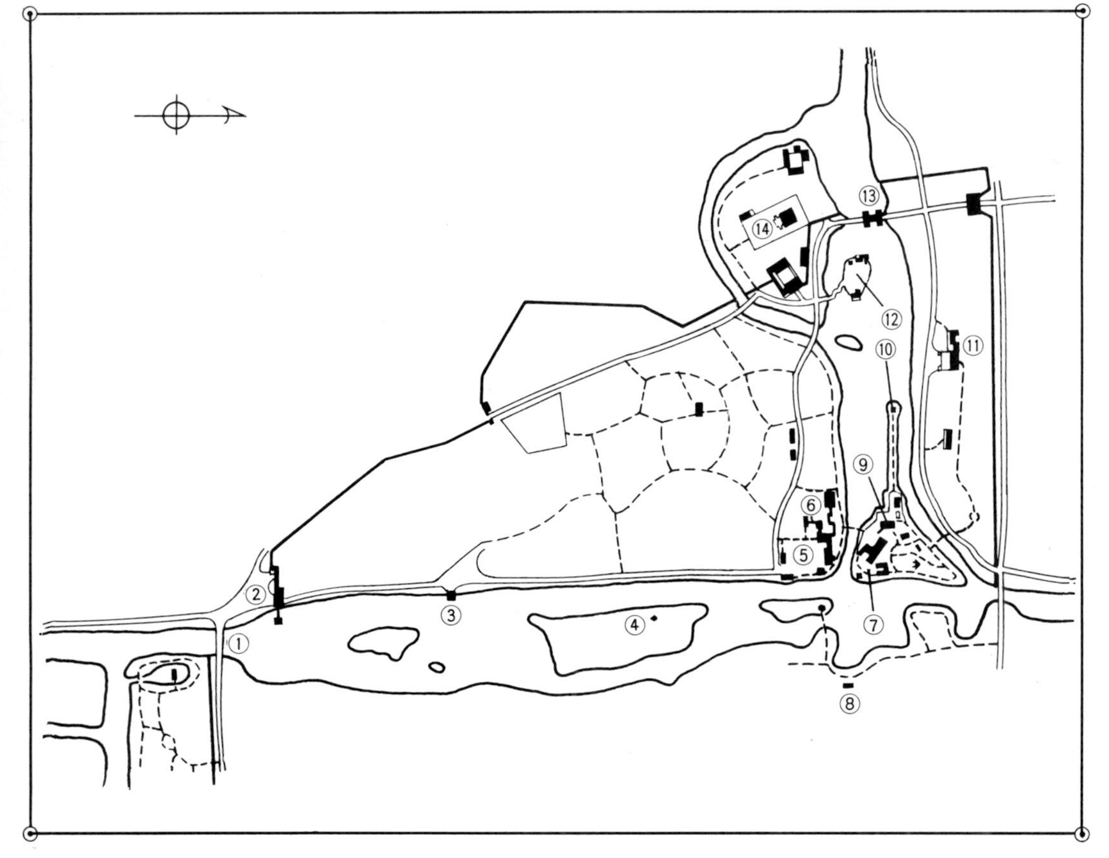

Slender West Lake

1. *Great Rainbow Bridge*
2. *entrance*
3. *Pavilion of the Causeway Amidst Spring Willows*
4. *Lotus Wind*
5. *Xu Garden*
6. *Carved Peak*
7. *Small Golden Mount*
8. *Year-round Misty Rainy Mansion*
9. *Carved Peak Chamber*
10. *Breezy Terrace*
11. *Big Osmanthus Hall*
12. *Island of Wild Duck House*
13. *Five Pavilion Bridge*
14. *White Dagoba*

154

154. White Dogoba and Five Pavilion Bridge

155

156

157

155. Slender West Lake colored by the setting sun

156. Wild Duck House. It is so named as it floats in the lake like a wild duck.

157. A view of the lake

158

159

160

158. Entrance gate of Little Golden Mount Garden. Inside the garden is a stalactite which was a tribute to the Song emperor Hui Zong.

159. The enclosed Little Osmanthus Garden. Inside the garden, rockeries, pavement and other built structures are brilliantly arranged, and the osmanthus flowers that grow everywhere in the garden cast an aromatic spell.

161

160. *White Dogoba and Five Pavilion Bridge framed in the moon gates of the Breezy Terrace*
161. *An exquisitely painted boat*

Level Mount Hall

Level Mount Hall is located to the northwest of the city in an area of hilly formations known as the Shu Hills. Extant ancient buildings include Temple of Great Brightness, Level Mount Hall and Level Distant View Mansion as well as the West Garden in the west. In 1980, the Memorial Hall of Monk Jian Zhen was constructed in the east. The whole scenic region of Shu Hills has long been called Level Mount Hall.

Great Brightness Temple was built in the Six Dynasties Period. In the Qing Dynasty its name was changed to Fa Jing Temple. The history of the buildings that exist now can be traced back to that era. These include the main hall, entrance gate and memorial arch, all along the main axis. Hanging at the entrance gate is a stone slab carved with the words ''Huai Dong Di Yi Guan (The First Temple of the East Huai District)''. This is a line from a poem by the Song Dynasty poet Qin Guan. From the Tang Dynasty onwards, poets and literati such as Li Bai, Gao Shi, Bai Juyi and Liu Yuxi all visited the area and left behind many poems in praise of its beauty. Great Brightness Temple was especially famous as it was the base where the high priest of the Tang Dynasty, Jian Zhen, preached Buddhism before he set sail for Japan. Since Jian Zhen was very successful in Japan, the Great Brightness Temple, as his base in China, also became well-known.

Level Mount Hall was built by the Song scholar Ouyang Xiu. It is situated to the west of Great Brightness Temple. The existing buildings include Ouyang Xiu Memorial Hall, Valley Forest Hall, and Level Mount Hall, all set on one axis. To the east of Great Brightness Temple is Level Distant View Mansion built during the reign of the Qing emperor Yong Zheng. Climbing the building one can have a beautiful view of the distant mountains.

The West Garden was built in the reign of emperor Qian Long of the Qing Dynasty. It is an affiliated structure of the temples and ancestral halls. Around the garden are rising and falling hills. At the center is a lake, the meandering edge of which looks natural and free. There are two islands in the lake, on which there are a boat house and Beauteous Spring Pavilion. To the northeast of the lake, amidst jade green bamboo groves and ancient woods are scattered little pavilions. To the southeast is Cypress Hall which is the main edifice of the garden. To the east of the lake is a miniature mountain on which is the sign ''Tian Xia Di Wu Quan (The Fifth Spring of the World)''. During the Tang Dynasty, the famed tea connoisseur Zhang Youxin named this spring the fifth best spring water for boiling tea, hence the name ''Fifth Spring.''

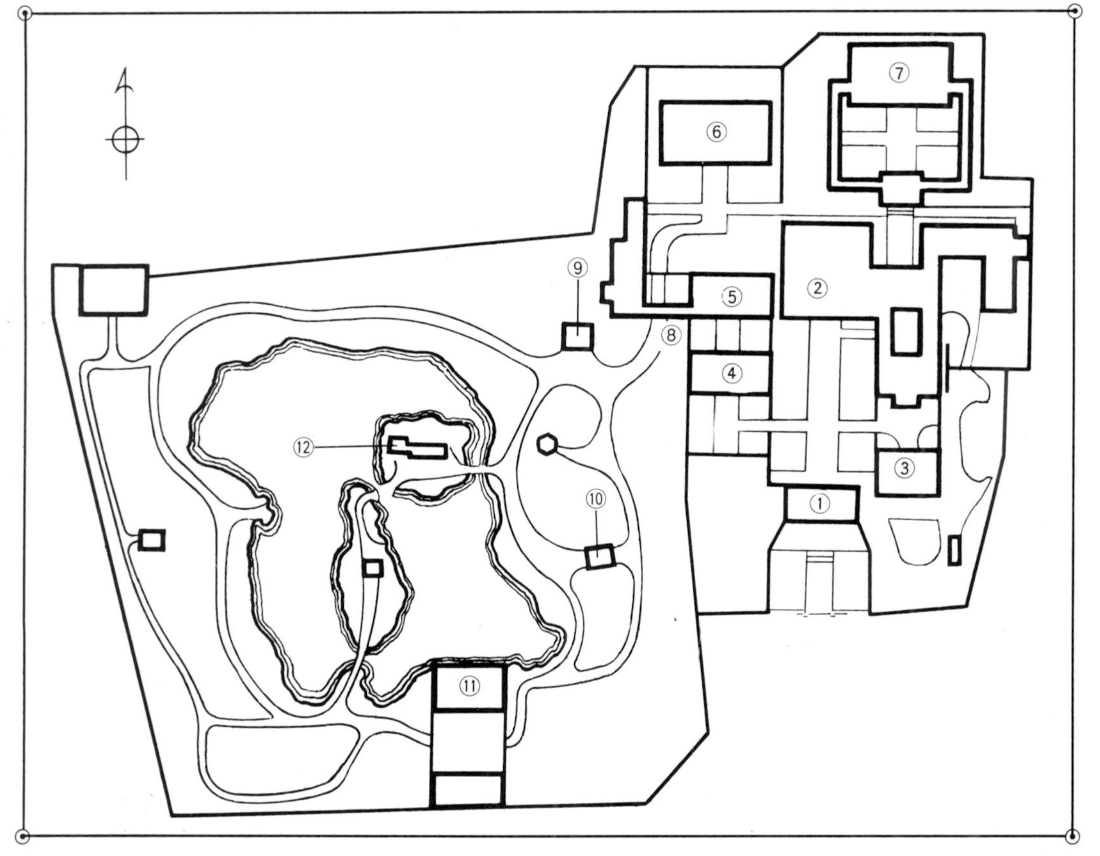

Level Mount Hall
1. *Temple of Great Brightness*
2. *main hall*
3. *Level Distant View Mansion*
4. *Level Mount Hall*
5. *Valley Forest Hall*
6. *Ouyang Xiu Memorial Hall*
7. *Memorial Hall of Monk Jian Zhen*
8. *entrance to the Fragrant Garden*
9. *Pavilion of Emperor Qian Long's Tablet*
10. *Pavilion of Emperor Kang Xi's Tablet*
11. *Cypress Hall*
12. *Boat House*

162

162. "The first temple in the East Hui District"

163

164

165

163. Exterior view of Level Distant View Mansion, built in the Yong Zheng era of the Qing Dynasty.
164. Stone steps near the entrance to the Fragrance Court, leading from the temple structures to the West Garden.
165. Cypress Hall in the West Garden

Golden Mount Temple

With a height of 60 meters and a circumference of 500 meters, Golden Mount lies to the northwest of Zhenjiang City. During the Eastern Jin Dynasty, the Temple of the Kind-hearted was built here. In Tang times, the temple was renamed Golden Mount Temple; during the Song Dynasty, the name of the temple was changed into Dragon Rove Temple; the name was again changed in Qing times to River and Sky Temple. However, the name Golden Mount Temple is far more popular.

Layer after layer of the component structures of the Golden Mount Temple are built according to the contour of the landscape and wonderfully encircle the top of the mountain, making it appear that the temple embraces the whole mountain. The mountain is thus called the Mountain of the (Golden Mount) Temple.

At the top of the mountain is the magnificent Benevolent Longevity Pagoda. The pagoda was built in the Qi and Liang Dynasties and was repaired many times. The present wooden pagoda is a piece of late Qing architecture. It is an octagon with seven levels. All around there are balconies which give a panoramic view of the surrounding scenery. To the east of the pagoda is Lofty Peak, beneath which is the terrace which is said to be the place where the Song scholar Yuan Tao sang the *Water Melody Song (Shui Diao Ge Tou)* while the poet Su Dongpo danced to the melody. To the west of the terrace is Seven Peak Pavilion, built on the site of Seven Peak Loft. The loft was supposedly the place where the monk Dao Yue had once interpreted for the Song hero Yue Fei the latter's dream.

Still extant at Golden Mount are the four ancient caves of the Monk Fa Hai, the White Snake, the Morning Sun and the Immortal. The caves of the Monk Fa Hai and White Snake are associated with the scene of ''The Water Inundating the Golden Mount'' from the folktale of *The Legend of the White Snake*.

On the southwest of the mountain is the Leng Qie Terrace, the place where the poet Su Dongpo wrote on Buddhist scriptures. The terrace offers an alluring vista: the sky and the river blend into one color on the distant horizon.

Half a kilometer west of the mountain is Cold Spring. Its water was considered by Tang Dynasty tea connoisseur Liu Bochu the best for boiling tea.

During the eighth year of the reign of Cheng Hua of the Ming Dynasty, a Japanese painter came to Golden Mount and painted the ''Painting of the Dragon Rove Temple at Golden Mount in the Yangtsze River Region of the Great Tang Dynasty''. The painting was such a masterpiece that everyone in Japan knew of it and the Dragon Rove.

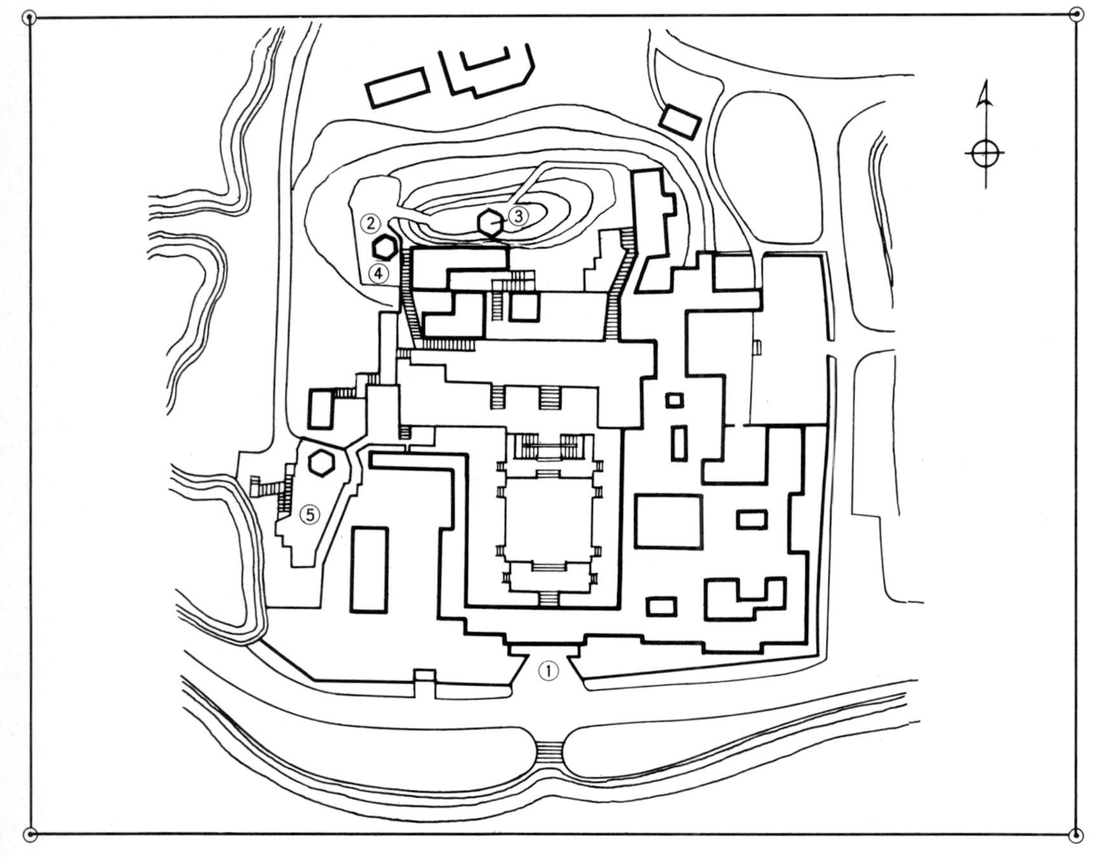

Golden Mount Temple
1. *entrance*
2. *Benevolent Longevity Pagoda*
3. *Pavilion for Viewing the River and Sky*
4. *Cave of Monk Fa Hai*
5. *Wonderful Terrace*

166

166. Entrance to the Golden Mount Temple

167

168

167. A pavilion at the entrance of the Ancient Immortals Cave

168. Exterior view of the White Snake Cave. Inside the cave the four words ''bai long gu dong (white snake ancient cave)'' in seal characters are inscribed on the wall.

169. Overall view of Golden Mount

169

West Lake

Hangzhou's West Lake is a world famous scenic spot. From its earliest development up to now, it has accumulated a history of over 2,000 years. West Lake was named Wulin Water during the Western Han; during the Tang Dynasty it was called Qian Tang Lake, as the Qian Tang River is nearby. However, as the lake is situated to the west of Hangzhou city, the common people have always called it Xi Hu, the West Lake. The lake is so beautiful that the Song poet Su Dongpo once compared it to the ancient beauty Xi Shi, and the lake is thus also known as Xi Zi Hu (Lady Xi Lake).

''Mountains in the clouds embrace it on three sides,

Hangzhou city beholds it at the opening.''

So it was written about West Lake which is surrounded by mountains in the north, west and south and Hangzhou city proper in the east. All of the mountains stand in elegant relief. The Gemstone Mountain in the north and Jade Emperor's Mountain in the south stretch out like two arms embracing the lake, this giving rise to the folktale of the ''Phoenix and Dragon Fighting For the Pearl'', the pearl being West Lake.

The present West Lake runs 3.3 kilometers at its longest distance from north to south and 2.8 kilometers at its longest distance from east to west, with an area of about 5.6 square kilometers. To the north of the lake stands Three Pools Mirroring the Moon, Lake Center Pavilion and Yuan's Mound compete for attention. Bai Causeway (so named in commemoration of the Tang poet Bai Juyi) lies tranquilly in the north with Su Causeway (built by Su Dongpo, a Song poet) in the west.

Because of continuous development throughout its history, West Lake boasts a great deal of valuable relics and historical sites. There are temples, ancestral halls, pagodas, stone inscriptions and grottos, forming many famous scenic points. The Southern Song painter Ma Yuan's celebrated scroll *The Ten Scenes of West Lake* successfully captures this beauty. The Ten Scenes have since been admired by visitors of all periods and the lake has become the most well-known scenic area in China and abroad. Though some of these scenes are nowhere to be found, people still come to search for their traces.

The attractions of West Lake can be grouped according to their locations: the lakeside area, lake area, mountain area and Qian Tang area. Of all the interesting places along the shore, Listening to Orioles Amidst Waves of Willows, Watching Fish in the Harbour of Flowers and Tomb of Yue Fei (a national hero of the Song Dynasty) are the most famous. In the lake area, Silent Lake Under the Autumn Moon, Mount Solitude, Xi Ling Seal Cutting Society (which exerted a great influence on the art of seal cutting in the late Qing Dynasty), Three Ponds Mirroring the Moon, Su Causeway in the Spring Morning, Bai Causeway, Yellow Dragon Cave, Monk Tao Guangs's Temple, Lotus in the Breezy Meandering Garden, Dragon Well, Jumping Tiger Spring and the Mist and Cloud Cave all do their best to enrapture the visitors. The Six Harmonies Pagoda, Nine Streams and Eighteen Rivulets, Clouds' Perch and Plum Dock in the Qian Tang area are also points of attraction.

Many historical figures left their names in West Lake. The Tang official Li Bi excavated the Six Wells. Bai Juyi, poet-official of the Tang Dynasty, built a causeway in the region. Though this causeway fell into oblivion, another causeway there is named after him now. Following the example of Bai, the Song poet-official Su Dongpo built the causeway which was to be named after him. The Song hero Yue Fei and Ming official Yu Qian had their tombs built in the region. The Windy Rainy Pavilion was constructed in memory of the heroine Qiu Jin of the Republic era. All these sites and the stories around them promote the development of the lake as a scenic region and enhance its attractiveness.

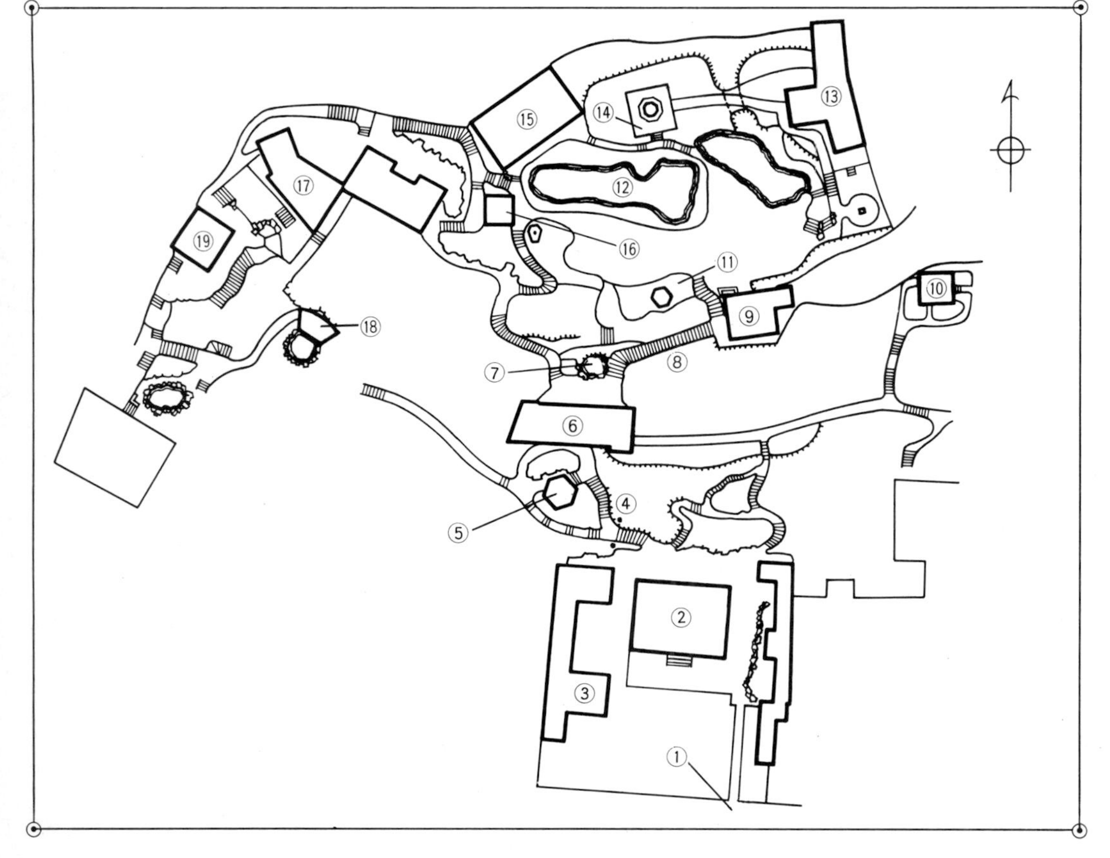

Xi Ling Seal Cutting Society

1. *entrance*
2. *Cypress Hall*
3. *Bamboo Pavilion*
4. *stone tablet bearing the name of the society*
5. *Shi Jiao Pavilion*
6. *Mountain Dew Pavilion*
7. *Seal Spring*
8. *Snow Path for Swan Geese*
9. *Four Light Pavilion*
10. *Living Quarters*
11. *Ti Xian Pavilion*
12. *Literary Spring*
13. *Ti Jin House*
14. *Pagoda of Hua Yan Sutra*
15. *Festive Mansion*
16. *Stone House of the San Lao Tablet*
17. *Hut of the Rustic*
18. *Ouyang Xiu Memorial Pavilion*
19. *Cloud and Crane Pavilion*

170

170. West Lake at dusk

171. The scenic spot of ''Ping Hu Qiu Yue (Silent Lake Under the Autumn Moon)'', a traditional site for enjoying the moon during the Mid Autumn Festival.

172

172. Overall view of the "Three Pools", an area marked by the three vase-shaped pagodas in the lake.

173

174

175

173. *Rockeries and lake in front of Wen Yuan Pavilion. The pavilion is one of the seven buildings where the **Siku Quanshu (Qing Encyclopaedia)** was housed.*

174. *A pavilion on Mount Solitude. On its lintel panel are inscribed the words "Xi Hu tian xia jing (Ultimate Beauties of the West Lake)"*

175. *Inside view of the garden of Xi Ling Seal Cutting Society. With its cave shrines and ponds cut out of natural rocks and surrounded by trees, it is a scene of archaic flavor.*

176

177

176. *One of the three vase-shaped pagodas marking the "Three Pools". The pagodas were orginally built by the Song poet Su Dongpo and reconstructed in the Ming Dynasty.*

177. *Exterior view of the garden of Xi Ling Seal Cutting Society. Founded by the Qing artist Wu Changshi, the society had exerted a great influence on the art of seal cutting during the late Qing period.*

178

178. Kai Wang Pavilion and Nine Turn Bridge in the scenic area of "Three Pools Mirroring the Moon".

179

181

180

182

179. *Garden of Yellow Dragon Cave*
180. *Rosy Cloud Cave, one of the most ancient caves in the West Lake scenic region. At the entrance is the Rosy Cloud Pavilion. Inside the cave are carvings of the Buddhist deities Guan Yin and the arhats.*
181. *Court of Jumping Tiger Spring*
182. *Dragon Well (Long Jing), famous for its spring water. The area where the well lies is famous for the production of* **longjing** *tea.*
183. *Heaven Emperor's Hall in Ding Hui Temple by the side of the Jumping Tiger Spring. In front of the hall are floating duckweeds.*

184. Sunset at West Lake

184

East Lake

Originally a stone pit, East Lake, after generations of development, is now a famous garden located outside the city of Shaoxing. The lake is long and narrow, its water green and clear, so clear that the bottom is visible. The rock mountain along the side of the lake emerges abruptly, forming a ''broken shore''. At the bottom of the mountain is a cave into which boats can cruise. In the lake itself is a causeway which is connected to the shore by a bridge, and highlighting the causeway are pavilions and trees composing a poetic scene. With its verdant greenery dancing in the breeze and its colorful flowers blooming in fragrance, with rare rockeries and crystal limpid water, the East Lake is one of the unique scenic spots in the east of Zhejiang Province.

185

185. The precipitous rock hill standing by the lakeside

186. The pavilion and bridge at the end of the long causeway

Thatched Hut of Du Fu

Du Fu, born in 712 A.D. at Gong Xian, Henan Province, is the greatest poet of the Tang Dynasty. In his lifetime, he traveled many places throughout the country and later settled in the capital Chang'an. In 755, the Rebellion of An and Lu broke out and he had to flee to Chengdu, where he lived for four years in a thatched hut. As a patriotic poet, he expressed for the people their grievances and many of his poems reveal faithfully the happenings of the time. So faithful and successful are his poems that they are called ''historical poems''. The influence of Du Fu on Chinese poetry is tremendous. To commemmorate this Saint of Poets, a memorial hall was constructed at his former residence near the Huan Hua River at West Suburb, Chengdu.

The original thatched hut where Du Fu actually lived fell into ruins after the middle Tang period. The present one is a reconstruction of the Northern Song Dynasty, the memorial hall was also constructed at the same time. During the Yuan, Ming and Qing Dynasties the compound was refurbished, and after 1949 it was further restored. Today, the compound of the Thatched Hut of Du Fu has become a little garden for people to relax in or show reverence to the great poet.

The Thatched Hut compound faces a stream with a hill at its back. Its structures make up two groups, one in the north, one in the south, running along a north-south axis. In the west is a pond fed by a clear stream with surrounding pavilions and bridges as well as galleries. In the east, the Thatched Hut Temple, now an exhibition room, makes up the major structure.

A stone bridge in the south will usher one to Da Xie Court, which is connected to the Historical Poems Hall by verandahs on its two sides. With a statue of the great poet housed in it, the Historical Poems Hall becomes the main structure of the compound. Going on, one will pass over a small bridge. The stream flowing beneath the bridge joins the waterside pavilion *(shui lan)* in the west with the Flower Path in the east. From the Flower Path one can reach the Thatched Hut Temple. The small bridge itself leads to the Faggot Door, the entrance to the north court. In the court's east is the Yi Shou Hang Pavilion while the Thatched Hut Study is in the west. Inside the main structure of Gong Bu Memorial Hall (Gong Bu being the official titles of Du Fu) is a clay statue of the Saint of Poets accompanied by statues of the famous Song poets Huang Tingjian and Lu You. Housed in the hall are also Ming and Qing stone inscriptions, among which are sketches of the Thatched Hut from the Qian Long and Jia Qing periods of the Qing Dynasty.

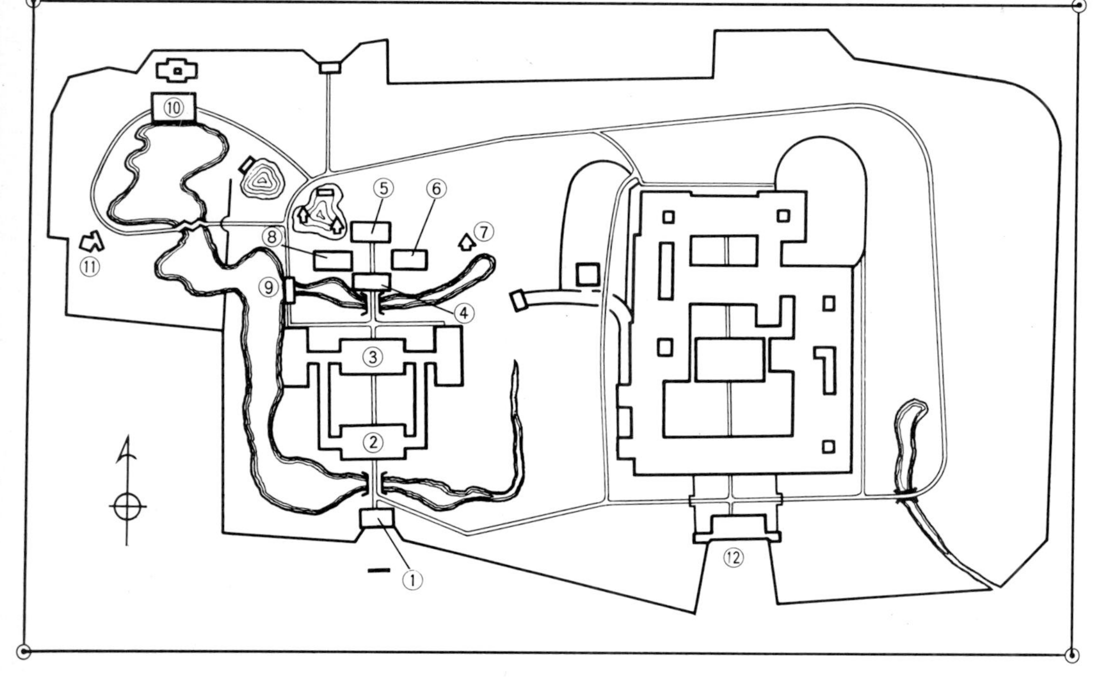

Thatched Hut of Du Fu
1. *entrance*
2. *Da Xie Court*
3. *Historical Poems Hall*
4. *Faggot Door*
5. *Gong Bu Memorial Hall*
6. *Thatched Hut Study*
7. *Pavilion of the Tablet of the Thatched Hut*
8. *Yi Shou Hang Pavilion*
9. *waterside hall*
10. *waterside pavilion*
11. *Overall View Pavilion*
12. *Thatched Hut Temple*

少陵草堂

188

189

190

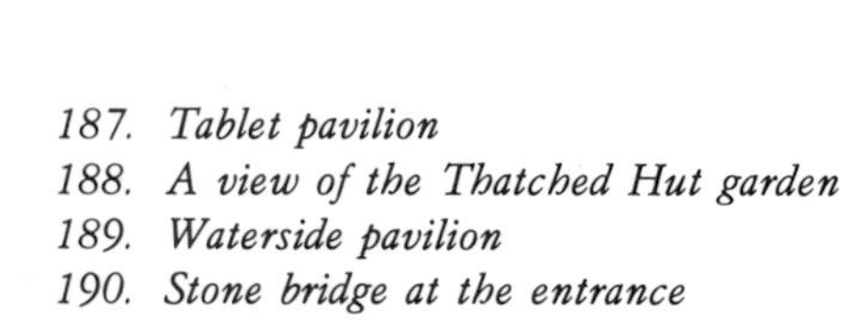

187. Tablet pavilion
188. A view of the Thatched Hut garden
189. Waterside pavilion
190. Stone bridge at the entrance

Memorial Temple of Jin

Memorial Temple of Jin is situated to the east of Xuan Weng Mountain, southwest of the city Taiyuan. A garden and memorial temple of very long standing, its earliest record is found in Li Daoyuan's *Notes on "The Book of Waters"* compiled during the Northern Wei Dynasty. It was originally the memorial hall of the Prince of Tang, a younger brother of Emperor Wu of the Zhou Dynasty.

The natural scenery here is very beautiful. In the garden there is a spring, the water of which flows through Zhi Bo Canal and Lu Bao River. From the Northern and Southern Dynasties to Ming and Qing times, the hall-garden underwent generations of development. Gradually it became a glorious recreational park with delightful buildings standing amidst a world of greenery. Ever since ancient times the second to fourth days of the seventh month of the lunar calendar have occasioned a festival to welcome the gods. At the festival, young men and women would come in crowds, enlivening the region with joyful conversation and excitement.

Three main clusters of buildings emerged in the course of the garden's development; the middle group being the most important. From the entrance in the east through Clear View Gate, Water Mirror Terrace, Meeting the Immortals Bridge, Golden Man Terrace, Dui Yue Square, Sacrificial Hall, Bell Drum Tower, Flying Beams Over Fish Pond (a four-way bridge spanning over a fish pond), and Heavenly Empress Temple form an orderly line on an east-west axis, with Heavenly Empress Temple as the focal structure.

Heavenly Empress Temple was built in the Northern Song Dynasty. The architectural form, Flying Beams Over Fish Pond in front of the temple, is the only one of its kind in China. Inside the temple are 33 painted figurines of Song maidens which, together with the Cypress of the Zhou Dynasty and Nan Lao Spring are called the Three Superlatives of Jin Memorial Temple. In addition, the stone inscription of the great Tang emperor Tai Zong's calligraphy is also an invaluable relic.

On the slope north of the Heavenly Empress Temple are such minor structures as Three Pure Ones' Cave, Lu Zu's Pavilion and Studying Platform. They ascend the slope one after another.

Among the structures of the north cluster, the Prince of Tang's Memorial Hall comprises the major one. Surrounding it are East Hill Temple, Guan Yunxiang Temple, Wenchang Hall and Heavenly Music Terrace.

The south cluster is composed of Sharing Happiness Pavilion, Three Immortals Temple, Nan Lao Pavilion, Mother of Seas Mansion and the Memorial Hall of Gongshu Zi, and on an earth mound in the south is a stupa. The plan of this cluster is free and vivacious, forming an organic whole with Zhi Bo River. The reflected images of pavilions and towers, glistening in the murmuring river, create a very special atmosphere for the garden.

191

191. The four way bridge spanning over the fish pond in front of Sheng Mu Hall

192

193

192. Spillways connecting Nan Lao Spring to Zhi Bo Canal. The spillways form different waterfalls with changes in the water level.

193. The archaic Sheli Shengsheng Pagoda. With a height of 38 meters, seven storied and octagonal, it is the tallest building in the temple compound.

194

194. Pavilion of Genuine Amusement and Untied Boat. One high, one low, the two structures make an interesting combination. From the pavilion one can enjoy the surrounding scene while in the "boat" one can dally with the water.

Wu Hou Memorial Hall

Wu Hou Memorial Hall was built in commemoration of Zhuge Liang (181-234 A.D.), alias Zhuge Kongming, a native of Shangdong. A celebrated statesman and strategist, he was the premier of the state of Shu Han (221-263) in Sichuan during the period of Three Kingdoms. He was also made the Prince of Wu Xiang and when he died, he was posthumously granted the title Zhong Wu Hou, ''zhong'' meaning loyal and ''wu'' meaning military, probably referring to his fief as well as his military talent.

Situated in the South Suburb, Chengdu, the hall compound occupies an area of 3.7 hectares. The exact date when the Wu Hou Hall was built is not certain. During the Ming Dynasty it was incorporated with the Memorial Hall of Emperor Zhao Lie of (Shu) Han. The compound, however, is still commonly known as the Wu Hou Memorial Hall.

The hall compound is made up of two clusters of buildings and a garden. The two clusters run on a north-south axis. The south front court is the Memorial Hall of Emperor Zhao Lie while to the north is the court where the Memorial Hall for Zhuge Liang is situated. Both courts are in a formal *sihe yuan* pattern with a central court enclosed by buildings on four sides.

Lying along the axis are the south main gate, the second gate, Liu Bi (Emperor Zhao Lie) Hall, a *guo ting* (a room connecting two major courts) and Zhuge Liang Hall. Displayed between the main gate and the second gate are six stone tablets among which is a Tang relic. Inscribed on the tablet is an epitaph praising Zhuge Liang written by premier Pei Du of the middle Tang period with calligraphy by the master calligrapher Liu Gongzhuo and inscription by Lu Jian, a famous carver. As the writing, calligraphy and inscription are all a *tour de force,* the tablet is called the ''Three Superlatives Tablet (Sanjue Bei)''. The Zhuge Liang Hall includes a study on its east side and a waterside pavilion on the west. The pavilion stands by a lotus pond, to the north of which is the Osmanthus House (Gui Hua Lou) and to the west the Floating Hall (Chuan Ting). Surrounded by buildings, the pond becomes a quiet court and is the main scenic spot of Wu Hou Temple.

Walking west from the Zhuge Liang Hall and passing a bridge and the Osmanthus House, one enters a path flanked by a red painted double rampart wall. The path, shaded by bamboo trees all along, is serene and peaceful. To the west of the path is the Hui Ling, a 12-meter-high earth mound where Emperor Zhao Lie is buried (According to the *Record of the Three Kingdoms* the emperor died at Bai Di City in 223 A.D. His body was sent back to Chengdu to be buried).

In the Wu Hou Memorial Hall are many lintel panel inscriptions *(bian er)* and couplets in memory of Zhuge Liang. The most well-known one by the Qing scholar Zhao Fan sums up Zhuge Liang's achievements:

> ''Once the heart is captured, rebellions will wane; since time immemorial true strategists have no desire for war.
> Not knowing the times, our judgement may err from truth. Following Zhuge Liang, great care should be practised by the rulers of Shu.''

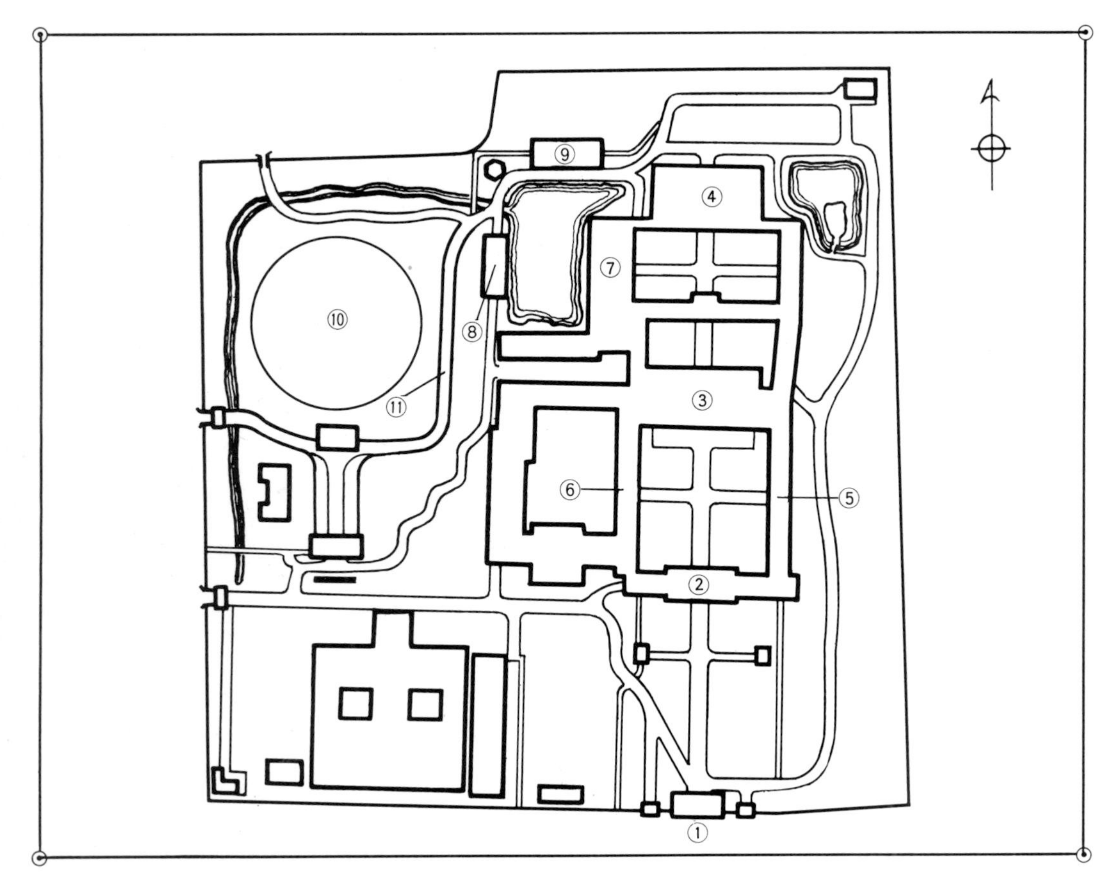

Wo Hou Memorial Hall

1. *main gate*
2. *second gate*
3. *Liu Bi Hall*
4. *Zhuge Liang Hall*
5. *Officials Gallery*
6. *Militarymen's Gallery*
7. *waterside pavilion*
8. *Painted Boat Hall*
9. *Osmanthus House*
10. *Hui Ling, Tomb of Emperor Zhao Lie*
11. *red painted double rampart wall*

195

196

195. Entrance hall
196. Floating Hall
197. The path flanked by a red painted double rampart wall

Five Spring Mountain

The Five Spring Mountain is situated in the old city site of Lanzhou north of the Gao Lan mountain's range, and is so named because of the mountain's five springs, namely, Gan Quan, Ju Yue, Mo Zi, Hui and Meng, Legend has it that Huo Qubing, the famous general who expelled the Xiongnu tribes from North China and thus secured the Han Dynasty, once stationed here.

On the east and west slopes of the mountain are gorges with splashing waterfalls. Known as the East Dragon Mouth and West Dragon Mouth, the gorges enliven the surrounding beauty, creating an air of vivacity in the midst of tranquillity.

During the region of Hong Wu of the Ming Dynasty, the first Temple of Worship and Celebration (Chong Qing Si) was built on the mountain. Since then, many more temples have been built, gradually turning the area into a scenic region. From the first to the tenth day of the fourth month of every lunar year, thousands of people flocked to the temples to celebrate the Buddha Washing Festival.

After the wars of the Qian Long and Tong Zhi periods of the Qing Dynasty, nearly all of the temples fell into ruins. Fortunately, they were reconstructed during the reign of Emperor Guang Xu. Liu Erxin of the early Republican era again refurbished the temples which have thus regained their old appearance. The present buildings are mostly constructs of the Guang Xu and early Republican eras.

The main temples of Five Spring Mountain are placed on a central axis which rises up along the mountain in a slight bend. The temples, standing together in tiers with their eaves overlapping each other, project a majestic image from afar. From the entrance arch, a flight of stone steps leads up to Profound Happiness Terrace, Butterfly Pavilion and Guardian God's Hall.

Guardian God's Hall is the only remnant structure of the Temple of Worship and Celebration. Inside the hall is a bronze statue of a standing buddha, and to the south are the Main Hall and Wan Yuan Pavilion. Wan Yuan Pavilion was first built at the compound of the old official examination center in the city proper, with the original name Bright Distant Mansion, and was moved to Five Spring Mountain later. To the west of Wan Yuan Pavilion is the site of Lighting the Lamp Temple on which now stand Heaven Palace and the Memorial Hall of Confucius' Disciples. To the southeast is Bell Tower in which is treasured an iron bell from the Tai He period (1201-1209) of the Jin Dynasty, and uphill from there are the Palace of the God of Literature (Wen Chang Gong) and the Temple of Souls Saving Buddha. Moving again to the southeast, one reaches the Thousand Buddha Pavilion situated high on a precipice. Below the pavilion falls the East Gorge where Meng Spring flows endlessly.

Among the various spots the West Gorge is the most attractive, brimming over with the atmosphere of a classical Chinese garden. To its north flows Hui Spring, beside which stand a small pavilion and a bridge. To the west of the gorge in the midst of thick woods is the Mani Temple. From here, a distant view of the Yellow River can be obtained and in the east appears the serene gorge. The scenes of the river and gorge comprise a view of unsurpassed beauty. Moving downwards, the West Gorge leads to the New Garden of Serene Green, built by the People's Republic modelled after the Small Heavenly Island Garden. Lying in the tranquillity of the garden are a pond and a pavilion.

199

200

198. *Guardian God's Hall. Inside is a Ming bronze statue of the Jie Ying Buddha, 1.5 meters in height.*
199. *Wan Yuan Pavilion.*
200. *Garden of Serene Green, a small classical garden built after 1949.*
201. *A view of Wen Chang Palace behind tree branches. Perched at the middle of the mountain, it offers an overall view of the surrounding scenery.*
202. *A bird's-eye view of the Mani Temple. The Yellow River is in sight to its north and to its south is a deep valley.*

201

202

Norbu Lingka

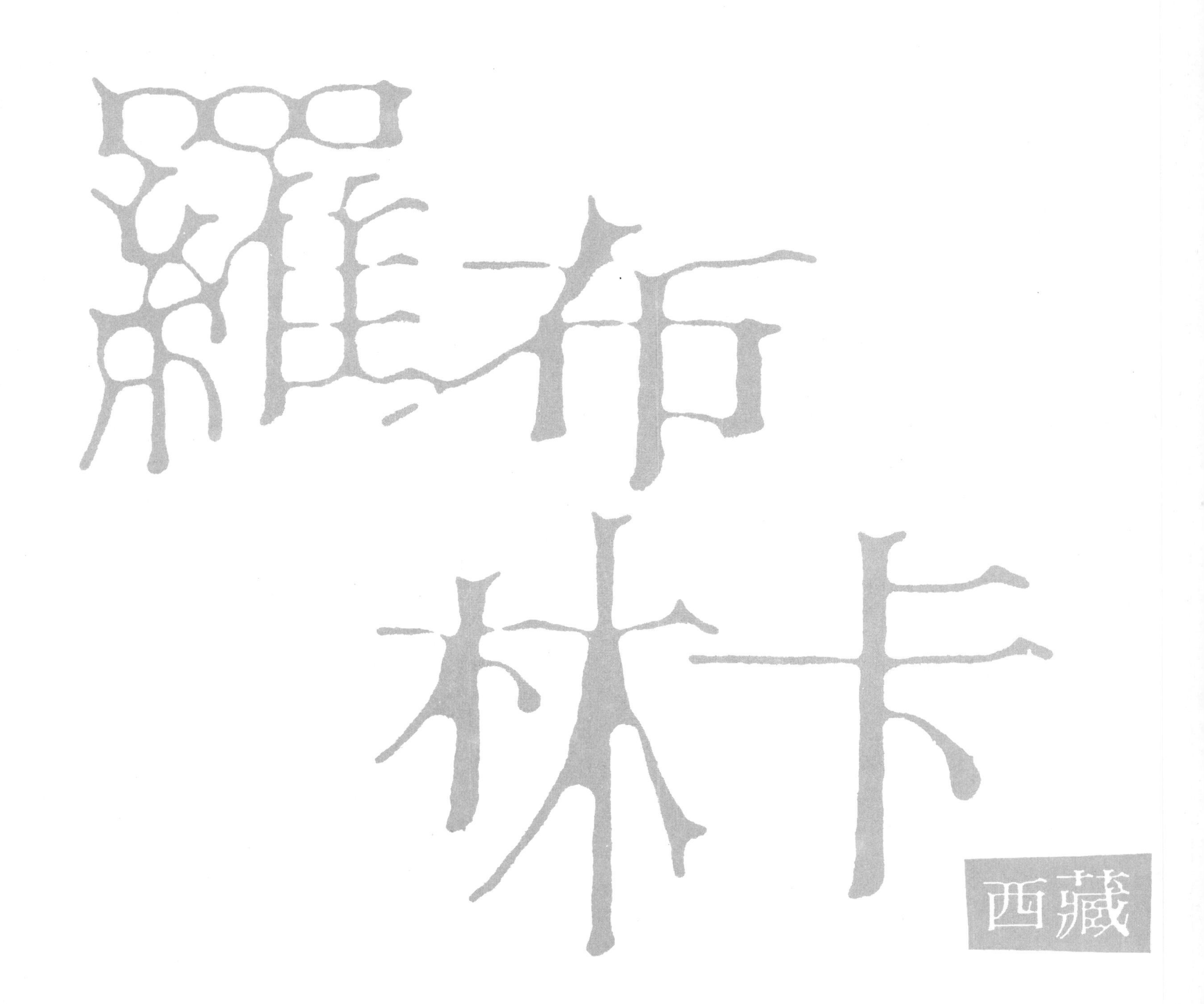

Norbu Lingka

In Tibetan the name Norbu Lingka means the "Treasure Garden". The former summer resort palace of the Dalai Lamas, it was originally a hall of repose after bathing, built by the Qing Dynasty Residential Officer in Tibet for the Seventh Dalai Lama. Continual extending and refurbishing during the following 200 years made it into the present large garden of about 360,000 square meters.

Inside the garden are large stretches of bushes and greensward which form several garden courts each with its own buildings as well as trees and flowers. This vast compound of forest and greensward constrasts strongly with gardens in inland China which are so designed that "a foot appears as a whole forest and mountain".

The earliest structure is the Gesang Pozhang Palace. The residence of the Seventh Dalai Lama, it was also the summer retreat for successive Dalai Lamas. Nearby, the Lake Center Palace comprises an artificial island and a large spring where the seventh Dalai Lama bathed. On the island are the small Lake Center Palace and Dragon King Palace. Silhouetted against the azure sky with their reflections in the lake, they make up the most beautiful scenic spot in the garden compound.

Comparatively larger in scale is the Jinse Pozhang Palace built by the Thirteenth Dalai Lama. With several groups of minor structures affiliated to it, it is free in layout, characteristic of Tibetan architecture. The sublime Dadanmijiu Pozhang Palace constructed after the foundation of the People's Republic, too, has preserved the Tibetan architectural style.

The Hall of Power Over the Three Realms (Weizhen Sanjie Ge) used to be the place where the Dalai Lama watched operas during the traditional Xuedun Festival. On that occasion, the common Tibetans would also be allowed to come into the garden to watch operas from behind the bushes in front of the hall. Today, all Tibetans are free to gather happily in the garden, set up their own tents, sing and dance and watch Tibetan operas to celebrate their festivals.

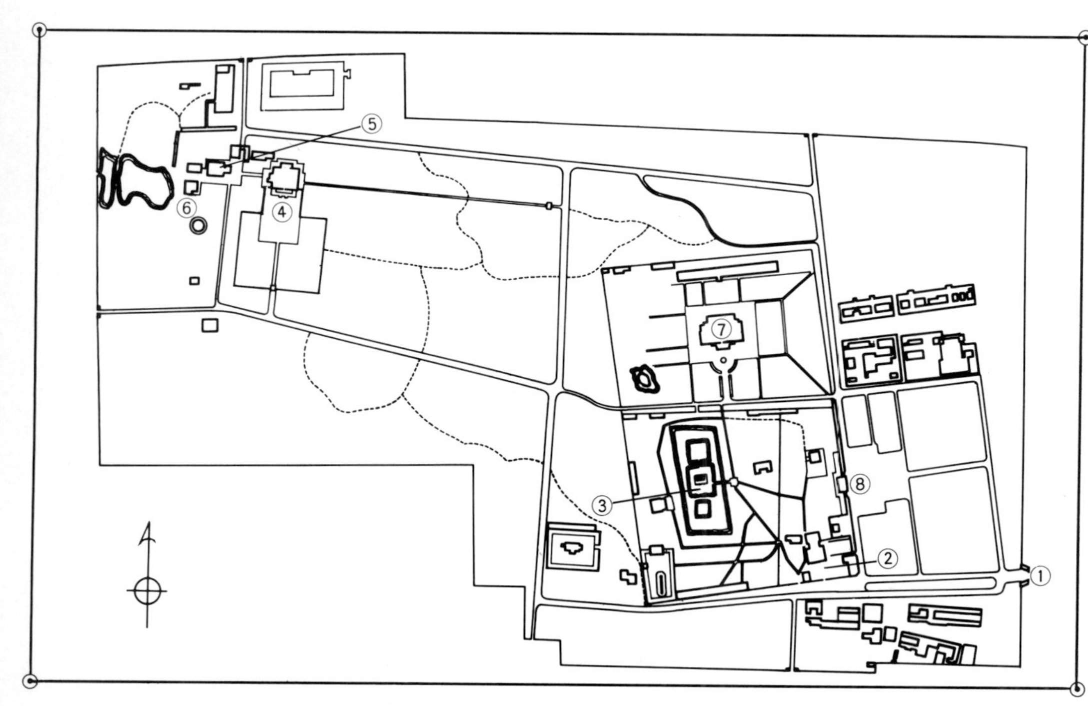

Norbu Lingka
1. *main entrance*
2. *Gesang Pozhang Palace*
3. *Lake Center Palace*
4. *Jinse Pozhang Palace*
5. *Gesangdeji Hall*
6. *Qimeiquji Hall*
7. *Dadanmijiu Pozhang Palace*
8. *Hall of Power Over the Three Realms*

205

206

203. Gesangdeji Hall. Constructed by the 13th Dalai Lama, its lower floor was the private treasure-house of Dalai, while the upper floor — the reception hall — was for important persons.

204. Qimeiquji Hall, the hall built by the 13th Dalai Lama during his latter years and is where he spent his remaining days. It is a comfortable living quarters built on a raised platform. Its lower level is just an empty shell, the hall itself framed with huge windows on its east and south sides.

205. A view of the garden in front of the Dadanmijiu Pozhang Palace.

206. A garden within the "Treasure Garden"

207

207. Exterior view of Dadanmijiu Pozhang Palace, the most recent construction in Norbu Lingka

208. Norbu Lingka is made up of large stretches of grove and greensward, typical of Tibetan gardens. Shown here is the entrance to the garden, flanked by trees.

209

209. An overall view of the Lake Center Palace. This site, originally the summer bathing place for the 7th Dalai Lama, later became the most beautiful scenic spot in Norbu Lingka with the construction of a lake and an island where the Lake Center Palace and Dragon King Palace are found.